CULTURE

A Survival Guide to Customs and Etiquette

DUBAI

Leena Asher

Marshall Cavendish
Editions

Published by Marshall Cavendish Editions
An imprint of Marshall Cavendish International
1 New Industrial Road, Singapore 536196

Other Marshall Cavendish Offices:
Marshall Cavendish Corporation. 99 White Plains Road, Tarrytown NY 10591-9001, USA • Marshall Cavendish International (Thailand) Co Ltd. 253 Asoke, 12th Flr, Sukhumvit 21 Road, Klongtoey Nua, Wattana, Bangkok 10110, Thailand • Marshall Cavendish (Malaysia) Sdn Bhd, Times Subang, Lot 46, Subang Hi-Tech Industrial Park, Batu Tiga, 40000 Shah Alam, Selangor Darul Ehsan, Malaysia.

Marshall Cavendish is a trademark of Times Publishing Limited

National Library Board, Singapore Cataloguing-in-Publication Data
Name(s): Asher, Leena.
Title: CultureShock! Dubai : a survival guide to customs and etiquette / Leena Asher.
Other title(s): Culture shock!
Description: Singapore : Marshall Cavendish Editions, [2016]
Identifier(s): OCN 956486768 | ISBN 978-981-4721-72-1 (paperback)
Subject(s): LCSH: Etiquette--United Arab Emirates--Dubayy (Emirate) | Dubayy (United Arab Emirates : Emirate)--Social life and customs. | Dubayy (United Arab Emirates : Emirate)-- Description and travel.
Classification: DDC 953.57--dc23

Printed in Singapore by Markono Print Media Pte Ltd

Photo Credits:
All photos from Leena Asher, except on page 47 (Roman Logov/ StockSnap.io)
• Cover photo: Nicolai Berntsen/ StockSnap.io

All illustrations by TRIGG

Culture shock is a state of disorientation that can come over anyone who has been thrust into unknown surroundings, away from one's comfort zone. *CultureShock!* is a series of trusted and reputed guides which has, for decades, been helping expatriates and long-term visitors to cushion the impact of culture shock whenever they move to a new country.

Written by people who have lived in the country and experienced culture shock themselves, the authors share all the information necessary for anyone to cope with these feelings of disorientation more effectively. The guides are written in a style that is easy to read and covers a range of topics that will arm readers with enough advice, hints and tips to make their lives as normal as possible again.

Each book is structured in the same manner. It begins with the first impressions that visitors will have of that city or country. To understand a culture, one must first understand the people—where they came from, who they are, the values and traditions they live by, as well as their customs and etiquette. This is covered in the first half of the book.

Then on with the practical aspects—how to settle in with the greatest of ease. Authors walk readers through how to find accommodation, get the utilities and telecommunications up and running, enrol the children in school and keep in the pink of health. But that's not all. Once the essentials are out of the way, venture out and try the food, enjoy more of the culture and travel to other areas. Then be immersed in the language of the country before discovering more about the business side of things.

To round off, snippets of information are offered before readers are 'tested' on customs and etiquette. Useful words and phrases, a comprehensive resource guide and list of books for further research are also included for easy reference.

CONTENTS

Preface	vi
Dedication	vii
Map of Dubai	ix

Chapter 1
First Impressions   1

At The Airport	2
A Global City	3
Safety in Dubai	4
Language	5
Getting Around	5
Weather	7
The Emirati Culture	9
Wardrobes	9
The Coffee Culture	11
Knowing Dubai	12

Chapter 2
Land and History   19

The Beginning	20
Leadership	21
The Government	23
Geography	24
Religion	26
Flora and Fauna	26

Chapter 3
Emiratis and Expatriates   29

Population	30
The Arabic Community	32
Arabic Homes	34
The Expatriate Community	36

Chapter 4
The Melting Pot   37

Islamic Greetings	38
The Society	38
The Grassroots Expat	39
The Changing Tides of Dubai	41
The Road Ahead	45

Chapter 5
Settling In   48

Before Moving to Dubai	49
Visas and Permits	51
Accomodation	55
Your Family	62
Pets	63
Banking and Money Matters	64
Costs of Living	76
Telecommunications	80
Education	81
Moving Around	83
Health Care	93
Registering Births	96
Getting Married	97
The Legal System	102

Chapter 6
The Food of the World Comes Here   107

Cuisines and Tastes	108
The Local Cuisine	111
Being A Guest	114
Inviting Your Friends Home	116

Chapter 7

Enjoying Dubai   118

A Top Tourist Destination   119
The Party Never Stops   120
Shopping   121
Experiencing Ramadan   129
Festivals   131
Local Folklore   131
Exploring Dubai   132
Activities Around Dubai   134
Dubai's Hidden Secrets   148
Tourist Must-Do's   154
Enjoying Dubai with AED 10   157
The Nuts and Bolts   158
Living Like A Dubaian   161
Sports in Dubai   168
Cinema   175
Eating Out   175
What's New   176

Chapter 8

The Language   180

History of Arabic   181
Arabic Language
Entertainment   184
A Bilingual City   184
Learning the Local Language   185

Chapter 9

Working in Dubai   186

Work Culture   187
Landing that Dream Job   191
Recruitment Agencies   193
Emiratisation   194
Economy   195
Starting a Business   205
Charity and Volunteer Work   206

Chapter 10

Fast Facts   208

Famous People   211

Culture Quiz   215

Do's and Don'ts   219

Glossary   221

Resource Guide   225

Further Reading   232

About the Author   233

Index   234

PREFACE

Writing *CultureShock! Dubai* was both a fulfilling and educational journey. It was such a satisfying experience to write about Dubai, the city I was born and brought up in, the city where I feel the safest in the world, the city I call home, the city I hear about when I travel, the city where the world comes, the city that outshines the rest of the region by leaps and bounds. When I travel outside Dubai and make friends, people are excited to know more about Dubai. I have welcomed several of them when they come here as tourists and I take pride in seeing how much they enjoy spending time in this city.

I have witnessed the city rising from the sands of the desert to the world-class city it is today. We have grown up together, Dubai and me. I counted the floors as Emirates Towers was being constructed and thought, this is going to be the tallest building in Dubai. Very soon, I was counting the floors as the construction of Burj Khalifa began.

Throughout my journey of writing this book, I have come to have a lot of respect for the leadership, the culture, the perfect life that Dubai tirelessly tries to create for all the people who step into this city, whether they are visiting Dubai for a day, a week or have been working here for several years and generations.

Dubai is my home and this is where I will always want to live. Having travelled around the globe, I consider Dubai home because it provides safety and security to me and my family, and a quality of life that I see unmatched anywhere else.

DEDICATION

*Dubai has been shaped as a dream
unfolding from the vision of His Highness Sheikh
Mohammed bin Rashid Al Maktoum.*

CultureShock! Dubai *is my dedication to His Highness
Sheikh Mohammed bin Rashid Al Maktoum,
the one man whose single, focused dedication
transformed the merchant transit city into a world-class
city that rivals its counterparts like Paris, New York and
London. His Highness Sheikh Mohammed bin Rashid
Al Maktoum's focused vision revolutionised Dubai; both
locals and expatriates are equally grateful.*

The magnificent Burj Khalifa.

MAP OF DUBAI

FIRST IMPRESSIONS

❝I want Dubai to be a place where everybody from all over the world meets each other, don't think of fighting or hate, just love it, enjoy their sport, and that's it.❞

**— His Highness Sheikh
Mohammed bin Rashid Al Maktoum**

AT THE AIRPORT

Whether your aircraft touches down at Dubai in daylight or at night, you are surely in for a treat. The one word I hear even residents say as they arrive in Dubai is "Wow!" This is usually people's first impression of Dubai.

Unless you are from one of the 33 countries eligible for a visa on arrival, you will require a pre-arranged visa to enter Dubai. Any hotel, tour operator or employer can arrange the visa for you. Don't get intimidated by seeing an Arab at the immigration counter. Most of them speak English and are always ready to help visitors. The world-class airport and duty free shops will leave you reaching for your wallet immediately and mind you, this is just the beginning.

Owing to its strategic location, Dubai is less than a four-hour flight to and from almost half of the world's population. The Dubai airport holds the position of the world's number one airport in handling passenger traffic of 75 million in 2015. With 100 airlines connecting 240 destinations around the world to Dubai, this is the city most passengers want to transit at or visit.

Nationalities That Get Visa on Arrival

Nationals of the Arab Gulf Co-operation Council (GCC) member states (Bahrain, Kuwait, Qatar, Oman, and Saudi

Arabia) do not need a visa to stay in Dubai. Expatriate residents (of specific professions) of GCC countries can obtain a non-renewable 30-day visit visa upon arrival at Dubai Airport.

British Citizens: Residents of the UK, with the right to abide in the United Kingdom, may obtain a free visa on arrival, which is valid for 60 days and can be renewed for an additional 30 days. Holders of the British Overseas Citizens Passport, who not have the right to abide in the UK, will also obtain the free visa.

Nationals of 33 countries getting a 30-day visa on arrival: France, Italy, Germany, The Netherlands, Belgium, Luxembourg, Switzerland, Austria, Sweden, Norway, Denmark, Portugal, Ireland, Greece, Cyprus, Finland, Malta, Spain, Monaco, Vatican City, Iceland, Andorra, San Marino, Liechtenstein, United States (US), Canada, Australia, New Zealand, Japan, Brunei, Singapore, Malaysia and Hong Kong. *(Refer to the section on* 'Visas and Permits' *in Chapter 5: Settling In for the different types of visas.)*

There are ample taxis and buses available outside Dubai airports. If you prefer, there are also taxis with lady drivers that are available upon request.

A GLOBAL·CITY

Dubai is home to over 2.4 million people from over 200 countries who reside in absolute harmony and understanding. A truly global city, Dubai strikes the perfect balance between its own conservative culture and the liberal lifestyles of the expatriates. Rather than being in competition, residents and locals complement each other in their ways of life. Many corporate organisations promote diversity and inclusiveness in their cultures for their staff to understand the societies and lives of their colleagues. It won't be a myth to call Dubai the world's most culturally diverse city.

Dubai is the second biggest emirate in the country of United Arab Emirates. The locals are called Emiratis. With the local Emiratis making up just below 15 per cent of the total population of the city, it is not hard to feel that the local-Islamic identity can be easily diluted under the sheer size of the expatriates almost feeling at home at Dubai. But ironically, this is not the case in Dubai. The next generation is evolving as they grow up in an international community at schools, malls, libraries, sports and parties. In keeping with the cultural values, traditions, language, cuisine and their family oriented personalities, locals balance their lifestyles between their parents and grand-parents, simultaneously raising their next generation with similar roots so they can identify their roots and know where they come from and belong.

In the words of His Highness Sheikh Zayed bin Sultan Al Nahyan, the late President of the United Arab Emirates, "He who does not know his past will certainly not understand the present. If a man knows the past, he will understand the present also and on that basis find out what lies in the future."

As the local Emiratis and the expatriates work on showcasing their best talents, cultures and products, pick up the Dubai Calendar and you can spot a variety of events from around the world all happening in Dubai.

SAFETY IN DUBAI
Dubai is often hailed for its impeccable safety record and the lifestyle it offers to expatriates and their families who can enjoy living here without fear of eve-teasing, robbery or crime. In contrast to other highly populated cities, Dubai has a high standard of safety, and violent crime is extremely

rare, but petty crimes do occur and normal precautions should be taken. It is not uncommon to see women walking, driving and taking taxis and travelling around the city after dark. Women on their own are not considered to be targets or at risk. However, it is advised to use common sense in dressing with respect to the local culture. When expatriates leave their homes vacant during the summer holidays for their vacations, burglaries can occur. It is good practice to advise the local security when you expect to be away. The key to surviving Dubai is staying safe. Stay safe when you are out on a girls' night out, stay safe when you have had a few drinks, stay safe not to mess with others, stay safe in public places. This will convert you from a newbie to a real Dubaian. Before you know it, you will be advising your family on what to expect in Dubai.

LANGUAGE

Although Arabic is the national language, English is more widely spoken in the city. Spot the written Arabic on the sign boards on the roads. Apart from Arabic, other languages spoken around by the expatriates are Hindi, Urdu, Bengali, Tamil, Tagalog, Persian, Chinese and Malayalam.

Bilingual signs at a waterbus station.

GETTING AROUND

To get around Dubai, most visitors get a Nol card – the prepaid travel card of the city. The word "nol" is an Arabic word for "fare" or "transport cost". Dubai is well-connected by its rapid transport system called the Metro, the driverless and fully-automated rail network. You can pick up your Nol card at any Metro station or online.

The Metro is the fastest way to get from point A to B. Like many other cities, Dubai roads get busy during office hours and trying to use a Metro or bus may not necessarily be a good idea. Unless you know how to squeeze your insides, it's not recommended to use public transport from 8:00 to 10:00 am and 5:00 to 7:00 pm. Airport terminals 1 and 3 have Metro stations connected to them. Make sure your hotel is close to a Metro station. You don't want to walk around a lot with your luggage. Taxis in Dubai are generally clean and drivers are well-trained to handle visitors. Your conversation with your taxi driver may be a better one than what you would have with a tourist guide. *(Refer to the section on* 'Moving Around' *in* Chapter 5: Settling In.)

WEATHER

The climate of Dubai is generally hot and humid, more so in summer. The city is warm most of the year. Winters in Dubai are considered the most pleasant time of the year in this city. By contrast, humidity levels rise to uncomfortable levels in summer. It's a tropical desert and that's a fact. A local joke that goes around is there is no other weather in Dubai; it's just hot, hotter or hottest. A long summer stretching from April to October keeps most people indoors. Once inside, it's hard for many to believe the outside temperature which tends to hit 50°C (122°F) in summer. Keep yourself well hydrated with a lot of cold water. It's thus natural, with a lot of time spent indoors, that Dubai has developed some of the world's best activities for indoor recreation. There are no summer rain showers or thunderstorms or hail storms in Dubai. Over 85 per cent of the local residents do not even own an umbrella!

During change of weather from spring to summer, low pressure areas develop, forcing strong winds from the north to Dubai. These winds are called Shamaal winds, "Shamaal" meaning "north" in Arabic. Shamaal winds that blow at a speed of 20 to 40 knots bring strong sand and dust storms along with them. Residents and visitors with dust allergies are advised to be cautious when they are outdoors during this time of the year.

From mid-March to mid-September is when the heat sets in, making the city hot and humid. The silver lining is that most of the city is air-conditioned and functions effectively and efficiently. All retail outlets, malls, clinics, hospitals, private and government offices, schools, trains, buses, bus stop shelters and all public places are air-conditioned to keep indoors comfortable for all in the city. Daytime temperatures can reach 50°C. There isn't much relief even after dark. Temperatures stay high throughout the days in summer. Dubai enjoys ample sunshine throughout the year from five in the morning until seven in the evening. There is no rainfall during these months. All schools in Dubai close for their annual vacation in July and August, which has a direct impact on the traffic situation in the city. With most families gone for holidays during this time of the year, the city is less crowded and relaxed during summer.

From October onwards the temperature begins to drop and gets only better from there till March. Temperatures move to mid-thirties during daytime and 25°C to 28°C in the evenings.

From the end of November until end of February is the best time of the year to visit Dubai. Daytime temperatures average around 25°C and evening temperatures can dip to as low as 10°C. January also brings some rainfall which makes most Dubaians very happy and cheerful. Parks and resorts get packed with families who plan all day long barbeques and picnics to make the most of the weather.

Although many may not find any need to open their winter wardrobes in Dubai, you may still notice women in boots, scarves and stylish winter wear. Dressing up in winter is a style statement that local Dubai residents never give a miss.

THE EMIRATI CULTURE

Dubai is an Islamic state and the social fabric of the city follows the Islamic way of living. Social mannerisms are held in high regard in the local culture. Meeting and greeting each other with respect and in the right way is considered important. Locals tend to exchange general pleasantries for a few minutes after meeting. An Arab name includes his own name, his father's name and his family name. E.g. The Crown Prince of Dubai is called His Highness Sheik Hamdan bin Mohammed Al Maktoum: Hamdan (being his first name), bin (meaning son of) Mohammed (his father's name) Al Maktoum (being the family name). Locals like to be addressed with their family name formally, e.g. Mr. Al Maktoum or Sayyed Al Maktoum (Sayyed meaning Sir). Local women can be address as Madame.

Men freely shake hands when they meet. However, local men and women do not shake hands. Foreign men should be mindful of shaking hands with local women. Many local women do not like to shake hands with men and this can include even educated and well-travelled women. A better alternative is to place your hand on your ear respectfully. Locals greet each other several times before settling down into a conversation. Customary pleasantries include enquiring about health, parents, family and children (pets are enquired). Be mindful not to ask questions about any females of the family. Greetings go on for a while. Hence, if you are going for a business meeting, expect greetings to go on for a few minutes before the actual conversation begins.

WARDROBES

Locals dress up according to Islamic values. Local women cover themselves from their hair to their feet. The hair is covered with a scarf called a *sheila*. The regular dress is covered with a black robe called an *abaya* that is worn over the normal clothes and is of full length, with full sleeves. Some local women also prefer to cover their faces. Ladies wear the *abaya* either for cultural or for religious reasons. The women who wear it for cultural reasons tend to experiment with a variety of fabrics, designs and cuts. Designer-labelled *abayas* and *sheilas* can cost from fifty to five thousand US dollars. Dubai has produced some of the finest *abaya* designers in the region. The designers develop their exclusive line of modern style *abayas*, prêt-a-porter and haute couture *abayas* with some of them extending their labels to customised *sheilas*, perfumes, and jewellery. Whether locals or expatriates, women in Dubai are expected to dress up modestly, wearing clothes that cover the shoulders, arms and legs. Ironically, in all-female company or inside female-only areas of the home, local women dress up quite provocatively, experimenting with a large range of Western wear that includes almost every Western designer label. Local females do not use swimsuits or bikinis. This is largely frowned upon. In the corporate world, local women are expected to wear *abayas* and *sheilas* over simple office wear.

Local Emirati men wear a loose long white robe called the *kandoora* made of fine white cotton or woolen fabric for winter wear. The head is covered with a white fabric called the *ghutra*. Every Arab country has its own distinctive style of *kandoora*. The differences are in the cuts of the *kandoora*, the collar shapes, to the colors of the headgear, the *ghutra*. In summer, a full white *ghutra* is worn and in winter colored checkered and printed woolen *ghutra* is popular. The *ghutra* is held in place by using an *agal*, a black rope that was originally made of camel tether. *Agal* styles also differ among the Gulf countries. For example, Qataris wear a more African-style *agal*, with two long "tails" reaching down the back. Among the Arab nations, the Omani style of wearing the *ghutra* is different than the rest. The *kandoora* is acceptable both for formal and informal settings. An outer cloak is called the *bisht*. In the earlier times, the *bisht* was worn by Arabs in winter. However, it is now worn mainly by the royals in formal settings like weddings or royal meetings. The *bisht* has real gold thread embroidery with expensive base fabric. The art of tailoring a *bisht* is a skill passed down from generation to generation. Traditionally, the *bisht* has two sleeves but it can be worn with only one arm through the sleeve and the other wrapped around loosely and tucked into the side.

THE COFFEE CULTURE

The coffee culture is both ancient and modern in the city of Dubai. Arguably, coffee originated in this part of the world and there is a new wave of artisan and boutique interest among both Emiratis and expatriates alike. With Dubai home to some of the best mall experiences in the world, you may find yourself skiing or sipping a hot mocha while the temperature outside hits 50°C. Bringing the world to Dubai, the coffee culture in Dubai is a live reminder of its cultural diversity.

An interesting twist is the addition of camel milk to the menu. Apart from being a local product, camel milk provides many health benefits, as it's higher in protein and lower in fat than cow's milk. The camel milk is further flavoured with cinnamon, honey or caramel to enhance its taste. This is available at the several outlets serving coffee from around the world, and is accompanied by many other activities. From coffee shops to *shisha* lounges, cake and confectionary boutiques, karaoke clubs, simulator games, pool and billiards tables, watching the latest cricket or football match together with family and friends or just lazing to have a cup of coffee as you watch the city pass by, this one activity will certainly please you.

On a bigger scale, Dubai has been holding the International Coffee and Tea festival for the last six years which incorporates several activities and events like Introduction to Coffee Roasting Techniques, Coffee Tasters Club networking, UAE Barista Championship and UAE Latte Art Championship in addition to the exhibition of coffee beans from around the world. The Dubai Tea and Coffee Festival is the only internationally-recognised trade event focused exclusively on coffee and tea in the Middle East. Last year, 6,500 visitors from 20 countries attended the event.

KNOWING DUBAI

Dubai like a grown up man, now in his 40s, with memories divided into old and new Dubai. Although there's nothing official about it, it's the old Dubai that treasures its stories, the forts, the experiences of the city as it grew from a pearl trading centre to the new Dubai, an extraordinary vision of a world-class city in the desert.

The old Dubai has been in existence since the start of Dubai itself and therefore displays the character, architecture, history and realities of times gone by. This is where the first traders arrived, import-export activities thrived, and pearl traders exchanged their deep ocean treasures for money.

A traditional house in the old part of Dubai. Traditional architecture often features wind towers, a structure built to provide ventilation and direct airflow to cool buildings.

The old parts of Dubai include Bur Dubai, Karama, Satwa and Jumeirah in the South and Deira, Hor Al Anz, Al Ghusias in the North.

With the massive influx of expatriates into the city in the early 1980s, the old parts of Dubai have become crowded. However, if you had to ask someone living in the old parts of Dubai, they would always prefer to continue living there. This is real, organic and nothing feels fake in this part of Dubai. Take a drive from Sheikh Zayed Road and within 30 minutes you will find yourself in New Dubai.

Abras, traditional small boats used to ferry people across the Dubai Creek. The fare is AED 1 (US$ 0.27).

Things To Do in Old Dubai

- Visit the Bastikiya Area and enjoy the local charm. The Majlis Gallery is Dubai's oldest art gallery founded in 1989 sits in the heart of Dubai's heritage circle.
- Take a ride in the local boat to get across the creek. Traditionally, the *abra* ride is how locals and residents crossed the creek. Today, the *abra* ride is a fun ride. *Abra* rides run from 10:00 am till 10:00 pm from the Bur Dubai Old Souq to Deira Old Souq.
- Eat at one of the local shacks that offer local, Persian, Indian and Pakistani meals and desserts. Recommended spots: Puranmal, Rangoli (Indian Food), Ravis's (Pakistani), Ostadi Kebabs (Iranian), Persian Cafeteria, Tasty bite (local takeaways).
- Buy a basil plant for as low as US$ 1.
- Walk around to pick up local souvenirs at the best rates.
- Explore the Dubai museum.
- Visit the local textile wholesalers and get dazzled by their endless collections.
- Buy local spices and herbs. Recommended visit: Madhoor stores at Cosmos Lane.

New Dubai

The new part of Dubai is where most newly arrived expatriates tend to spend more time. The DIFC, Dubai Marina, Jumeirah

The Walk at Jumeirah Beach Residences, a popular outdoor shopping, dining and entertainment promenade.

Lakes Towers, Greens, Meadows, Springs, Jumeirah Beach Residence, Dubai Silicon Oasis, Motor City, Arabian Ranches are some of the neighbourhoods where most expatriates live today.

Jumeirah Beach Residences, or JBR as it is called fondly, is a massive 2-km (6,562 ft) long waterfront residential and commercial development compromising 40 high-rise residential towers and hotels overlooking the Arabian Gulf. The Walk at JBR is lined with restaurants and retail outlets.

Night view of the twinkling, glamourous Dubai Marina, where yachts are moored.

Dubai Marina is one of the most sought after locations by new expatriates arriving to Dubai. Dubai Marina offers Riviera-style living in a modern setting, spanning an area of 4.6 sq m (50 million sq ft) with a large, 3.5-km (11,483 ft) long canal. The Dubai Marina high-rise apartments offer most residents the view of the Marina where yachts are moored. The Dubai Marina Walk is a popular dining location on weekends, offering restaurants serving world-class cuisine, shopping and entertainment. The Marina Mall is the local mall which is frequented by local residents. Dubai Marina Yacht Club is the authority for all operations and berthing in the Dubai Marina canal. Dubai Marina is inspired by the Concord Pacific Place development along False Creek in Canada. There are several cases of marine wildlife (especially whales and sharks) entering the Marina due to its connectivity to the ocean.

Jumeirah Lake Towers or JLT which is administered by DMCC (Dubai Multi Commodities Center) is a collection of 26 clusters, each hosting three towers, with each tower having its own name. JLT has been built around artificial lakes and landscaped parks. Walking to work and back home is a concept that works well in this neighbourhood as it has designated towers for commercial and residential use. Many professionals working in JLT prefer living in the same neighborhood for this convenience: to avoid traffic and the city rush.

The Greens is a neighbourhood of low-rise residential apartment buildings focused on creating a community and courtyard environment. With convenient amenities like swimming pools, gyms, restaurants and schools all within walking distance, The Greens is a popular neighbourhood for families with schoolgoing children.

Dubai International Financial Centre (DIFC) is a federal financial free zone established in 2004 to provide a platform for financial institutions and related businesses with infrastructure

The Dubai International Financial Centre, home to the Ritz-Carlton, art galleries, restaurants and service outlets.

benchmarked against international standards. The DIFC has its own legal system and courts distinct from those of the wider UAE, with jurisdiction over corporate, commercial, civil, employment, trusts and securities law matters.

CHAPTER 2

LAND AND
HISTORY

> ❝ Thirty years ago we had no buildings, and when we saw buildings in other countries we used to envy them and wonder how we could convince our people to be satisfied with what they had. ❞

— Late President of UAE, His Highness Sheikh Zayed bin Sultan Al Nahyan

THE BEGINNING

Dubai has been inhabited since 3000 BC by nomadic tribes of cattle herders. The Umayyad Caliphate spread Islam in the region. Dubai was first mentioned in the Andalusian-Arab geographer Abu Abdullah Al Bakri's *Book of Geography* in 1095 AD, although Dubai was dependent on Abu Dhabi until 1833 before its pearl industry was established. The earliest recorded history of settlements in Dubai dates back to 1799. In time, Dubai came to be known as a centre for trade and pearling. The rulers (Sheikhs in Arabic) made a deal in 1892 with the British, under which the United Kingdom agreed to "protect" Dubai from the Ottoman Empire. The tribe of Bani Yas led by Sheikh Maktoum bin Butti Al-Maktoum moved from their part of Saudi Arabia to the Dubai Creek to settle down close to this water feature.

In the 1930s, the thriving pearl industry of Dubai collapsed in the mist of the global Great Depression. The discovery of oil in 1971 brought about the boom in Dubai. In December 1971, Dubai joined the six other emirates to form the country of United Arab Emirates (UAE). In less than five years, the city's population more than tripled with the influx of foreign workers flocking into the city to take advantage of the growing trading hub and to work as part of this developing city. In

1958 when H.H. Sheikh Saeed bin Maktoum Al Maktoum passed away, Sheikh Rashid bin Saeed Al Maktoum became Ruler of Dubai. H.H. Sheikh Rashid al Maktoum is fondly remembered by the migrants who regard him as the driving force behind making Dubai a known city at the time when the world knew little about it.

LEADERSHIP

All that Dubai stands on today, undoubtedly, is the vision of this one man. His Highness Sheikh Mohammed bin Rashid Al Maktoum, the Ruler of Dubai, with a vision of the skies and even beyond.

His Highness Sheikh Mohammed bin Rashid Al Maktoum

Sheikh Mo, as he is fondly called by expatriates in Dubai, spoke about his vision for Dubai in an interview, as "the embodiment of confronting difficulties, overcoming obstacles and conquering the impossible". These words have held true ever since his office began. The ruler began his journey as head of the Dubai Defense in 1970s. His extraordinary vision brought to reality the formation of Emirates Airlines in 1985, the construction of Burj Al Arab in 1999, the creation of Palm Jumeirah in 2001 and the Dubai Metro in 2005, just some of projects that have one after the other, taken Dubai's position one notch higher, making it a world-class city. The Dubai Metro system is the longest automated rail network in the world, with 87 driver-less trains.

As Dubai prepares to achieve its golden jubilee in 2021, His Highness Sheikh Mohammed bin Rashid Al Maktoum's vision is already moving ahead with its agenda. Some of the top items are hosting Expo 2020 that will bring the world to

Dubai, where His Highness Sheikh Mohammed bin Rashid Al Maktoum promises to "astonish the world"; the Dubai Canal project; constructing themed parks in Dubai and most ambitiously, to launch its mission to Mars, making UAE the first Arab country to venture into this arena. His Highness Sheikh Mohammed bin Rashid Al Maktoum aims to build the best city in the world.

One of the initiatives taken by His Highness Sheikh Mohammed bin Rashid Al Maktoum is the development of online *majlis* at www.mbrmajlis.ae. The leader has taken the traditional *majlis* online, where the leader invites everyone who can offer ideas, comments and suggestions to strengthen the position of Dubai in various sectors and fields.

Inspiring quotes by His Highness Sheikh Mohammed bin Rashid Al Maktoum:

- "Absence of a competitor is one of the worst things a leader can face. It leads to a relaxed and a non-challenging environment."
- "Thinking collectively and having open dialogues with the team at work create new ideas and bring us closer to success."
- "Life is boring without challenges, and I fully trust in my team's ability to meet their challenge and lead us to global excellence."
- "We want everyone to work as one team to achieve the goal, with positive energy, strong determination and the belief that anything is possible."
- "The word Impossible is not in leaders' dictionaries. No matter how big the challenges, strong faith, determination, and resolve will overcome them."
- "A great leader creates more leaders and does not reduce the institution to a single person."
- "Our goal is to establish UAE as a successful global model combining: economic growth, energy sustainability and clean-safe environment."
- "It is easy to rule through fear, but it takes a rare leader to rule through love."
- "A few mistakes made by a person working productively cost far less than a person paralyzed by laziness or fear."

THE GOVERNMENT

Dubai is the second biggest emirate in the country of the United Arab Emirates (UAE). The country is made of seven emirates or states. Established on 2 December 1971, the UAE is a constitutional federation. The country enjoys full sovereignty and independence with its national flag, logo and national anthem. The UAE nationality is recognised internationally.

The Constitution explains the main rules of the political and constitutional organisation of the country. It demonstrates the main purpose of the establishment of the Federation and its objectives. It also elaborates on the major social and economic pillars of the Federation and stresses public rights, responsibilities and freedoms.

The UAE Constitution protects human rights and prohibits torture and various forms of inhuman and degrading treatment. It also prevents arbitrary arrest, search, detention, and imprisonment.

The UAE President heads the Federal Supreme Council and appoints the Prime Minister of the UAE. The Vice President assumes all authorities granted to the President during his absence. The Federal National Council (FNC) is the fourth federal authority in terms of order in the hierarchy of the five federal authorities mentioned in the Constitution. It comprises 40 members.

Spearheaded by His Highness Sheikh Mohammed bin Rashid Al Maktoum, Vice-President and Prime Minister of the UAE and Ruler of Dubai, as part of the Government's dynamism, UAE now has a Minister of Happiness and a Minister of Tolerance. UAE also has a brand new "UAE Youth Council" that will bring together young men and women under the age of 22 to serve as advisors to the government of UAE on youth issues. UAE Council of Scientists has also been formed that will "review national policy for science, technology and innovation". These new Ministries and councils will take UAE to its next level of progress and efficiency.

The Smart Dubai Government Initiative
The Smart Dubai Government initiative is a pioneering initiative by the Dubai Government that aims to provide innovative smart government services to all segments of the society, including a wide range of online services for businesses and residents of Dubai. Several government run services are now online in the form of websites and apps like smart parking (for paid parking service) and smart Salk (for toll gate service). As simple as the tasks may seem, the Smart Dubai Government initiative has a huge mission ahead: to plan, process, implement, supervise and oversee the transformation of government services.

The Minister of Happiness
While taking her oath, the Minister of Happiness of UAE Her Excellency Ohood Al Roumi made a bold and cheery statement from the word go, literally wearing her mission statement on her sleeve. The new Minister of Happiness wore a Lanvin necklace over her *abaya* that read "Happy" as she stepped into the new role. The brand new Minister's role is to implement and oversee national projects that improve the quality of life and general wellbeing of the UAE's citizens and residents.

GEOGRAPHY
Dubai, in the northeast of the UAE, is the second largest emirate of the country, located on the Persian Gulf with an urban area of 3,885 square sqkm (1,500 sq miles). Dubai

shares its borders with Abu Dhabi in the south, Sharjah in the northeast and the Sultanate of Oman in the southeast. However, Dubai has managed to increase its size with the addition of reclaimed land and man-made islands like The Waterfront, the three Palms, The World and The Universe.

A very fascinating fact of Dubai is the Dubai Creek, a swallow narrow water inlet in the Persian Gulf that divides the city into two parts – one that stretches into the North into Deira and into the South into Bur Dubai. The North part of the city covers locations starting from Deira to Hor Al Anz, Mamzar, Ghusais, Muhaisanah, and Al Nahda, ending at Sharjah. There are no borders between Dubai and Sharjah. The South of the creek at Bur Dubai (the inner circle call this the happening part of the City) covers areas from Bur Dubai, Karama, Oud Metha, right into the new side of Dubai and Dubai's life line highway of Sheikh Zayed Road, sprawling over Jumeirah right to Abu Dhabi. The new part of Dubai is filled with tourist attractions and home to any world-class brand for clothes, leisure, entertainment and hospitality. A leadership with a unique vision of seeing Dubai as a world-

The famous Atlantis Hotel, an impressive sight set on the iconic Palm Jumeirah island with unblocked views of the Arabian Gulf.

class city is home to unique architecture and construction projects like the Palm Jumeirah, an artificial collection of islands in Dubai laid out to resemble a palm tree. Dubai has its own mountain range called the Hajar Mountains. Hajar means "rock" in Arabic.

Due to the city's unique geographical location, it enjoys a strategic position which allows it to connect to all local Gulf States, as well as to East Africa and South Asia. Dubai's nearest seismic fault line, the Zagros Fault, is 200 kilometres (124.27 miles) from the UAE, which means it is unlikely to have any seismic impact on Dubai.

The strategic location of Dubai was soon identified which led to the development of Port Rashid followed by a much larger Jebel Ali port with an annual cargo tonnage of 13.6 million TEU (in 2013), a large number of which are earmarked for re-export.

RELIGION

Islam is the official religion of Dubai and the United Arab Emirates. If you stay long in Dubai, you will get used to the Adhan, the call for prayers as Muslims are called to pray at the Mosque. Muslims pray five times each day, facing Mecca. In all hotel rooms in Dubai you will find a sign that points towards the direction of the holy city of Mecca. You will also find prayer halls and rooms in office buildings, malls, hospitals and clinics and at the airport. It is not considered good manners to walk towards or stare at someone who is praying.

FLORA AND FAUNA

Dubai is basically a desert but you will be amazed at the well planned landscaping of the city. While the desert area has wild grasses and desert hyacinths, the acacia and ghaf trees can be seen in the mountain areas. Don't be surprised as you see

The picturesque, stunning Jumeirah Mosque, one of the most photographed sights in Dubai, and one of the only mosques open to organised tours for non-Muslims.

several exotic floras that are imported to the city in its parks.

Some of the desert animals include the Bedouin's best friend, the camel, and the odd houbara bustard, caracal, desert fox, hedgehogs, falcon and Arabian Oryx. Crawling creatures like black widows and the redback spider are part of the local fauna.

Dubai lies on the migration route for many animals, hence it becomes a seasonal home for migratory birds like flamingos, and yellow billed storks and reef herons. In fact, there is a flamingo nature reserve off Oud Metha road if you would like to view the bird in its natural environment. Take the Oud Metha road and turn left at the BuKadra Interchange on to the E44, where, after a few hundred yards, you'll need to park on the left side of the road.

Dubai waters are home to over 300 different types of fish. The aquatic fauna include crabs, jellyfish and ray fish. The favourite fish is hammour which is also a staple seafood for the locals. Other common sea life animals include jellyfish, crabs, dolphins and turtles. If you fancy discovering the local flora and fauna, the Dubai Desert Conservation Reserve offers a professional safari guide through the desert where you can spot the Arabian Oryx, gazelles or maybe even the rare Gordon's Wildcat.

CHAPTER 3

EMIRATIS AND EXPATRIATES

RESIDENTS

INDIANS 2 MILLION
PAKISTANIS 1 MILLION
FILIPINOS 1 MILLION
BENGALIS 600,000
IRANIANS 400,000
NEPALIS 150,000
CHINESE 200,000
SOUTH AFRICANS 100,000
CANADIANS 50,000
AMERICANS 40,000
RUSSIANS 18,000
AUSTRALIANS 7000
EUROPEANS 10,000
BRITISH 240,000

TRIGG

POPULATION

Dubai Statistics Center (DSC) carries out daily and monthly estimates of the population permanently residing in Dubai within the geographic borders of the emirate, whether they are Emiratis or Non-Emiratis. The current population count of Dubai is 2,468,381. Only around 15-20 per cent of Dubai's population is local Emirati. Most of the population comes from other countries, such as India, Pakistan, Bangladesh and the EU. Out of this, 69 per cent of them are male and 35 per cent female. In 1995, Dubai's population was under 700,000. Owing to the rapid investment and business opportunities making Dubai an attractive immigration destination, the population has been growing steadily at 5 per cent per annum. Dubai is expected to be home to over 3.4 million people by 2020. An interesting rise compared to a starting population of about 300,000 when the country was formed in 1971. The population of Dubai has been consistently growing at five per cent per annum. Dubai is home to about 40,000 Americans and about 50,000 Canadians who work mostly in white collar jobs.

The biggest expatriate group living in Dubai comes from India. Indians in Dubai are spread in almost every industry from business to professional to blue collar labourers. Dubai is home to over 2 million Indians, making it the largest immigration base comprising 42 per cent of total population of UAE. Out of the 2 million Indians, about 40 per cent hail from the South Indian state of Kerala, which benefits from the remittances made by the Keralites back home. India is Dubai's second largest trading partner, exporting foodstuff, spices and textiles, among other fast moving products to Dubai. Indians live in almost every part of Dubai with a major concentration in the old Dubai areas of Deira, Bur Dubai, Karama and Al Quasais.

The second largest groups of expatriates in Dubai hail from Pakistan, making up about 21 per cent of Dubai's population. Coming from different parts of Pakistan, Dubai is the largest non-resident base for Pakistanis involved in businesses, professions and blue collar jobs around the city.

Filipinos make the next 21 per cent of Dubai's population with a majority of them in either the service industry or professional jobs.

China is Dubai's top trading partner and has a rapidly growing Chinese population in the city. Dragon Mart 1 and 2 are better known as Chinese markets, which showcase and sell exclusively Chinese products to the local market. There are over 200,000 Chinese living in Dubai. Being a stone's throw away from Dubai, Iran has over 400,000 people mainly owning businesses in Dubai.

Dubai is home to over 7,000 Australians and 10,000 European expatriates. There are several French training centres in Dubai. Alliance Françoise is located in Oud Metha in the heart of Dubai and offers diversified certification language courses in French.

Other nationalities in Dubai include 600,000 Bangladeshis, 150,000 Nepalese, 18,000 Russians and about 100,000 South Africans.

THE ARABIC COMMUNITY

The locals in Dubai are called Emiratis (derived from Emirates).

Islam is the way of life in Dubai, deeply rooted in its cultures and the lifestyles of both the nationals and expatriates alike. A good example of this is the culture of tolerance showcased by local and expatriates alike during the holy month of Ramadan. Dubai is very known to be tolerant to other religions and cultures.

You may notice how Emirati men greet each other by touching their noses to one another. Don't laugh and don't react as this a traditional greeting among Emirati men. The regular and normal greeting is the international handshake which works well with all men. Do not shake hands with any woman, Emirati or expatriate, unless she extends her hand for a handshake. The same applies for a foreign woman meeting an Emirati man. Do not shake his hand unless he extends his hands for a handshake. The concept of personal space in the Emirati culture is quite different from its European counterpart. Standing or sitting too closely to the personal space of the opposite sex is not seen with approval.

The Emirati society is basically male dominated. The head of a family is mainly the oldest male whose age is equated to experience and wisdom, followed by the eldest son or eldest brother.

Visitors to Dubai are expected to be aware of its Islamic traditions. You may find things that are absolutely acceptable in Western culture to meet with very little tolerance here in Dubai. A good example of this is women's dressing, which in the Western culture has no barriers, living by the "have it, flaunt it" attitude of dressing. However, in Islamic society, women are expected to dress modestly. You may see Muslim women cover their hair and wear full sleeves even in summer.

Most malls and public offices here have stickers at their entrances reminding women to keep their arms and legs covered. However, there is relative tolerance for dressing up in hotels, bars and at hotel pools. There are no nude beaches in Dubai.

Women are highly respected in Islam. Since Islam is the official religion of Dubai, women are respected and always expected to behave modestly. It is always a good idea to request permission when taking photos with local women. Taking photos of Arab women without their permission can be punishable. Touching women is not well tolerated. A smile and conversation are much better.

As mentioned in Chapter 1, the men traditionally dress up in a white gown robe called the *khandura* with a white headdress called the *ghutra*. The women wear a comfortable fitting black robe called an *abaya* which is worn over their regular clothes. The women cover their heads and some also their faces, with a scarf called a *sheila* or *hijab*.

The city nonetheless is known to be the entertainment capital of the Middle East. Dubai is home to the world's best bars and pubs. Name it and find it here in Dubai. Cavalli, Armani, Neos, 360, they are all here. Alcohol consumption is permitted to non-Muslims within selected and licensed outlets. There is zero tolerance towards drinking and driving in the city.

When you have a meeting set up with an Emirati, be mindful of the laid back culture. Do not get offended if your guest arrives even 15 minutes late. It's a way of life and not an intentional delay. If you ever receive an invitation to attend an Emirati wedding, be aware that functions for ladies and men are held separately. No men are allowed inside the ladies' functions and vice versa. One of this author's personal experiences has been a refusal from the bride's mother to be photographed, as she thought that the author would share her picture with family and friends, which was unacceptable.

A beautifully decorated traditional *majlis* for greeting guests, commonly seen in local family compounds.

ARABIC HOMES

Unlike most of their Western residents, the local style of living is with extended families. Culturally and traditionally, Arab live together with their parents and extended families which calls for them to have big sized homes or several small villas in the same compound. It is not uncommon to see three to four generations living under the same roof, a huge kitchen where family meals are prepared and mealtimes being family affairs. Locals prefer to live in houses compared to apartments. Locals are provided land and loans by the government to build their homes. Generally, locals do lease part of their villas to expatriates. As a result, foreigners in Dubai have a wide range of villas, town houses and apartments to choose from.

Local family compounds have a shared *majlis* – the traditional formal meeting area of the house for visitors. Many

compound houses are built in the *majlis* style, with an area opening immediately from the front door where the men meet visitors and sit with them. The rest of the accommodation is from the sides or rear. In local houses, women don't open the front door and are not to be seen unless the visitors are close relatives. The compound of several detached villas normally has a big parking space to accommodate the several cars owned by the families sharing the compound. The idea of living together or close to each other comes from the tribal mindset of the locals, where keeping the brood together was important. There is also a perspective of convenience attached to it. Men of the family gather for Friday prayers and walk to the nearest mosque together to pray. In Ramadan, the fast is broken together as a family meal.

THE EXPATRIATE COMMUNITY

UAE's population as of Dec 2015 is 10,359,000. Expatriates make up over 85 per cent of this population. Ask anyone who has visited Dubai and they will wish to be here again at least once in their lifetimes. Offering the best of both the East and West, the city has all it takes to make life safe, comfortable and convenient. Fondly called the Vegas of the Middle East, expatriates here find themselves in a fantasy land: big homes, clean streets, tax-free incomes, world-class cuisines, international communities, theatres and lots more. For the thousands of expatriate professionals whose work brings them to Dubai, moving to Dubai was the best decision.

Dubai is a big shopping party, an exciting holiday destination, a great work experience, a thriving business hub and lots more to anyone who is drawn to its broad daylight and glamorous evening skies. Whether it is a small town family or a cosmopolitan world-travelled one, Dubai makes it comfortable for everyone to settle down in a safe, relaxed environment. With the advent of the Internet which keeps families and friends connected everywhere in the world, it is easy to get on Skype and WhatsApp as you discover this city and make new friends. Use the Internet to find out what's happening in the city. This is a good first step to finding friends with common interests and interests and passions. The websites www.meetup.com and www.timeoutDubai.com make good starting points. Since a large part of the population is expatriate, it is easy to make friends even if you think you are shy.

CHAPTER 4

THE MELTING POT

> *7 billion people.*
> *One bridge that connects us all.*
> *Hello Tomorrow.*

— **from Emirates Airline's marketing campaign**

ISLAMIC GREETINGS

Always begin by greeting the most senior person in the room first. Muslims greet each other by saying "Assalamo Alaikum", which means "May peace be upon you and may God's blessings be with you". The reply to this is "Walaikum Assalam". Then shake hands and say pleasantries like how you are, how your family is, how your children are. Locals exchange pleasantries several times before settling down to a conversation. Unlike the Western professionals, Emiratis do not like to be addressed by their first name but rather as Mister or Madam or Your Highness or Your Excellency.

THE SOCIETY

The local Emirati society has the family as the core of its social unit. The fabric of this unit is held close, with honor, respect and pride. The family and kin's honor are paramount for all. The local Emirati society places great emphasis on the emotional, physical and sociological support systems that are created by large families. The society is basically patriarchal and hierarchal, with fathers or the eldest male members leading the household decisions.

THE GRASSROOTS EXPAT

As you know by now, the locals make just about 15 per cent of the total population of this city. The rest are expatriates from over 239 countries. Out of the 85 per cent expatriate population, about 25 per cent of them are grassroots expatriates who have been in Dubai for over 40 years, setting up businesses and making it their home. Although they renew their visas regularly, citizenship is not granted to expatriates irrespective of the length of their stay in the city. Although the UAE is dependent on foreign skilled and unskilled labour to support the machinery of the country, permanent residency is not offered to any expatriate. Grassroots expatriates have lived in Dubai most of their lives, own property, are involved in running small, medium and large scale businesses and hold high profile jobs. Having lived in the city for over 40 to 50 years, they hope they can live in Dubai permanently, in the country they love and have grown to call their home.

One such grassroots expatriate, Mr Bhatia says, "Our community, the Thathai Bhatia community, has been around in Dubai for over 113 years, from the time Dubai didn't have its own administration. Our visas were issued by the authority called the British Embassy. Trade and banking back then were administered by the Khoja and Kutchi communities and the Indian Rupee was the official currency used in Dubai. The early Indians to arrive in Dubai traded in gold and garments. Many of us began with very little money in our pockets and have grown with this city. Our children have attended schools here and thanks to god, many Dubaians are spread all over the world in well-placed jobs."

Most grassroots expatriates hail from India. Special areas, such as the Souq al Baniyan, are where they began their journey. The journey continues even four decades later.

Rizwan Sajan, Founder and Chairman of Danube Group, is another homegrown success. Sajan attributes his decision to move to Dubai in 1991 to his wife, who had the conviction that Dubai was the ideal ground for her husband to explore his entrepreneurial efforts. From humble beginnings on the streets of Dubai to a magnificent business empire that ranges from building materials to food and beverage to fashion to real estate, Sajan is a firm believer  that determination, along with ground zero learning, are key factors to success. Proving his spouse's decision right, he is largely inspired by H.H. Sheikh Mohammed bin Rashid Al Maktoum, the ruler of Dubai, for constantly providing a sound and conducive environment for businesses to thrive in Dubai. Sajan sees himself moving with the tides in Dubai, growing along with the city one day at a time.

Mounir Bouaziz, a Tunisian-French expatriate who heads a major oil company in Dubai, moved to the city with his spouse and two schoolgoing children in 2004. Mounir and his family have lived in various cities like Amsterdam, Oman and Gabon before moving to Dubai. Although the family spent a Christmas break in Dubai before making the big move, Mounir still experienced the challenge of finding a school suitable for the needs of his children. With the children settled down, the family swiftly settled into their life, making new friends easily around the city.

Mounir has high regards for the Flag Carrier of Dubai, Emirates Airlines for providing great connectivity from around the world into Dubai. He fondly recalls flying from Houston and yet being able to join the family for dinner all in the same day.

Thirteen years on, Mounir's next assignment takes him into another city, but he plans to retire in Dubai for the comfort, convenience and modern lifestyle available in the city. "My wife says Dubai makes me look ten years younger!" says Mounir.

The other type of expatriates are called "transitional expatriates" who arrive here for a fixed period of time and are conscious that Dubai won't be their home but they will be here for some time and move on. Even such expatriates cannot but feel at home, make friends and feel attached to the warmth of the city.

THE CHANGING TIDES OF DUBAI
Dubai and the World

Dubai is an exemplary example of great PR. A global city, a venue for most international events, moderate, liberal and yet cultural, Dubai strikes the perfect balance for both visitors, residents, locals and neighbours. This is achieved with the help of the Department of Tourism and Commerce Marketing and Emirates Airlines, which has taken Dubai to the world stage.

Emirates Airlines sponsors the AFC Champions League, AFF Suzuki Cup, and is the primary sponsor of the football clubs AC Milan, Arsenal, Hamburger SV, New York Cosmos, Paris Saint-Germain and Real Madrid apart from sponsoring the umpires as the official partner of the International Cricket Council. Emirates Airlines also sponsors several horse racing events like Dubai International Racing Carnival, Melbourne Cup Carnival and the Australian Jockey

Club. Emirates Airlines is the major sponsor of the Emirates Team New Zealand challenger to the 34th America's Cup in sailing and also sponsors Collingwood Football Club in the Australian Football League. Dubai has been seeking to reduce its dependence on oil and increase its visibility on an international level through tourism.

New Ways of Life

Many call it the Manhattan of the Middle East, others call it a work in progress. There are several waves that are changing the tides of Dubai.

With the advent of satellite television, a whole new world of information has opened up to the Emiratis in the last 10 years. This has profoundly affected their lives. From experimenting with different cuisines and travelling around the world, to exploring other cultures, ways of living, lifestyles and ways, Emiratis today are much more travelled, better-educated, forward-looking, open-minded and ready to meet the expectations of their leaders.

Khulood Al Qayed is an Emirati who holds a Master's degree in Public Relations. Khulood is symbolic of today's Emirati woman, someone who considers herself a complete personality as she balances the several roles in her life, being a daughter, a wife, a mother and a sister.

"I returned to work four months after giving birth, the idea of which is not just unusual but even surprising in many Emirati households," says Khulood. "While I am at work, my baby is taken care of by my in-laws. This helps me to feel relaxed that my baby is in reliable hands. My husband is an equal partner to me in many ways, perhaps unlike the men in the previous generation. He takes pride that he has a qualified spouse who is at par with her peers in an international professional environment."

The Emiratis take pride in their culture and their Islamic roots. The Emirati attire is a living tradition in itself. You may notice several Emirati women working at both government and private offices putting on the *abaya* (the black robe that is worn over their clothes) and covering their hair with the *sheila* (the headscarf).

The role of women is now changing in the society of Dubai as they are considered partners in progress. The leadership of Dubai has a strong conviction that women are truly a success story to be celebrated. Although the history of Arabic women is conservative, the changing lives of women in Dubai are an example of how the dedicated leadership is empowering and changing the lives of women in Dubai, taking their roles in the society to a different level. Women in Dubai are being encouraged to enroll into schools, universities and for higher education, and they have done so successfully. Women have achieved outstanding progress, accounting for over 70 per cent of university graduates. The leadership has taken a lead in the region to empower women politically and, over the past few years, women have begun to more visibly contribute in the political arena. Women in Dubai are now participating actively in the political sphere through representation in the Federal National Council (FNC) and local consultative councils, as well as in the formation and shaping of public policy through active roles as ministers in the Federal Cabinet. The government's serious commitment to ensure that women participate in decision-making at the highest levels was reinforced by the Cabinet reshuffle of His Highness Sheikh Mohammed bin Rashid Al Maktoum, increasing the number of female ministers to four.

There are many more Emirati females who continue to strive to bring glory to the country.

Apart from the changing role of the females in the Emirati society, the city is standing witness as the local population explores the world outside their homes. Regularly planned job fairs are attended by enthusiastic Emirati freshmen and women, keen to enter the workforce. The Friday ritual of an extended family lunch following the Friday prayer is kept

alive in many households, with the evening spent at the malls now. With both partners working during the week and spending weekends outdoors, interaction with neighbours is not like in the past, where neighbours lived like family. Weddings are now often held at high-end hotels, preserving the beauty of the culture, music and traditions.

THE ROAD AHEAD
Expo 2020

Dubai won the bid to hold Expo 2020, beating Yekaterinburg in Russia, Izmir in Turkey and São Paulo in Brazil, making it the first Middle Eastern destination to host the event. UAE selected the theme "Connecting Minds, Creating the Future", with sub-themes being Sustainability, Mobility and Opportunity. On 27 November 2013, when Dubai won the right to host the Expo 2020, fireworks were displayed from the world's tallest building, Burj Khalifa. All educational institutions in Dubai enjoyed a national holiday following the announcement. Sheikh Mohammed bin Rashid Al Maktoum promised that Dubai would "astonish the world" in 2020. Dubai expects to create 277,000 jobs in the city as it prepares to stage the world fair. Over 25 million visitors from 180 countries are expected to reach Dubai to witness the greatest show. The world's tallest commercial tower, Burj 2020, is planned in honor of the World Expo 2020. The brand new logo for Expo 2020 was revealed in March 2016.

Dubai Plan 2021

The forward-looking leadership of Dubai has already put together its plan after 2020. Dubai's focus for 2021 is on the people and creating a "City of Happy, Creative and Empowered People". According to its website, the aims of

Dubai Plan 2021 are to inspire:

- Educated, Cultured and Healthy Individuals: Individuals who take care of their own wellbeing and that of their family through proactive measures to manage their health and enhance their skills and ability to contribute to the economy and society of Dubai building on their solid education and cultured upbringing.
- Productive and Innovative in a Variety of Fields: Individuals who strive to succeed, are financially self-sufficient, and embody the mindset and disposition of entrepreneurs and responsible citizens.
- Happy Individuals Proud of Their Culture: Individuals who are generally satisfied with their life in Dubai, confident about their future and proud of their cultural origins.
- People are the Cornerstone for Dubai's Development across all fields: Emiratis men and women playing an important role in the development of Dubai and filling critical roles across various sectors including social, economic, and urban.

Aerial views of the city that has seen stunning growth in the last decades. Not surprisingly, Dubai attracts talents from all over the world.

CHAPTER 5

SETTLING IN

❝Socialise like brothers, do business like strangers.❞

— **Arabic proverb**

BEFORE MOVING TO DUBAI

Most corporate organisations that expect to receive expatriate employees into Dubai use the services of relocation consultants to ensure a smooth relocation transition and settling down process in Dubai. Since Dubai receives many new expatriates on a regular basis, there are several relocation consultants operating in the city. The consultants offer lots of practical information on the small bits of settling into the city.

A pre-moving checklist:

- Legal documents: Ensure that family members have valid travelling documents (passports) with sufficient validity.
- Certificates that require attestation and ministry endorsements like school and university degrees, school transfer certificates, project and work experience certificates and marriage certificates.
- Medical preparation: Handle the family's dental care, ensure the family's medical history documents are up-to-date, originals and copies of vaccination certificates and birth certificates.
- Banking and insurance: Update your new communication address to your banks, pension authorities and insurance company.
- Pets and birds: Pets may need to be quarantined.
- Other arrangements: Arrange "powers of attorney" if you require someone to handle any affairs in your absence. Also check if you need an international driving license (remember that it is valid for only one year and it cannot be renewed; you must apply for it again).
- Cancellations to be done: Electricity, gas, oil, water, telephone (also your mobile) and Internet. Cancel your subscription to any clubs, associations, courses, newspapers, etc. Close your bank accounts unless you think that you will use them, and redirect your mail through the Post Office.

Working with packers and movers: be prepared with a list of items to be packed and shipped. Many moving companies will be able to come to your home to assess the labour requirement, quantity of packing material, space required by your items in the shipping container and time required for the move and will be able to offer a quote accordingly. Try to get a quotation from a few for comparison of quality of service, price and time management. Items like expensive pieces of art, pianos, snooker table, etc. may require insurance to be arranged prior to shipment.

For individuals or families planning to relocate into Dubai, moving companies have arrangements with shipping companies for "group tonnage", which means they combine cargo from several families to maximise the space used in the container, thereby being able to offer a competitive shipping rate to all customers. A bit of creative, advanced planning ahead helps to take advantage of this option.

Besides the price, it is also important that you check what

services the different removal companies provide. Some will only load in and load off your boxes; others will provide you with boxes and containers for you to pack; others will pack, load, transport, unload and unpack all your stuff (while you give them instructions from your armchair). Some might even help you with the cleaning and tiding up, so be nice to them. Check if they transport pets, heavy items (such as pianos) and fragile items (chandeliers, vases, ceramics, etc.). You should also make sure that the company gives you a guarantee of refund in case they do not succeed in transporting your stuff and that you get their maximum shipping time in writing.

Jewellery (including ornaments, solitaires, and designer pieces) are to be insured and carried personally. If you have fragile or valuable items you should insure the load at once. Keep in mind that most insurance companies will cover your stuff with the condition that people from the removal company packed it (if you do not get the full service it is possible that you will be uncovered). The cost of the insurance is of 1 per cent or 2 per cent of the load's total worth, depending on the amount of cover that you get.

It is also a good idea to retain the services of a relocation company once you arrive in Dubai. They can help with the unpacking of boxes. In case you are staying at a hotel on arrival, you may need to arrange for your possessions to be stored at a moving company's storage area until you have rented your home. Get help from your employer or colleagues to negotiate the storage rate as this can vary on location.

VISAS AND PERMITS
The Employment Residence Visa
The most important visa of Dubai is the residence visa which entitles the holder to reside in Dubai for a specific period

of time. Types of residence visas depend on your duration and purpose of stay in Dubai.

The employment residence visa in UAE is issued to all persons employed in Dubai. Other than some exempt companies, all employees in Dubai carry a labour card called "Bataqa". Once approved, the employment visa is printed and stuck like a sticker on the passport. The employee is required to clear a medical screening, which includes a blood test and chest x-ray (if requested). Once cleared, the visa is stamped in the passport run by the Department of Health. A patient found to have tuberculosis or hepatitis is not given visa approval. Check with the UAE Embassy in your country or with your employer for the documents required to apply for your visa. The requirements are updated from time to time.

A male employee can go on to sponsor his wife and children. Since the judicial systems follow the Islamic law, the father is expected to sponsor his family. Female employees cannot sponsor their spouses or children. On humanitarian grounds, some female professionals are allowed to sponsor their families. The applications are assessed on a case-to-case basis by the immigration authorities. Parents can sponsor a male child until he turns 18 and a female child until she is married.

Employment visas carry a validity of three years and can be renewed easily. The retirement age in Dubai is currently 60 years.

Other Types of Visas For Entry Into Dubai

Dubai offers different types of visas depending on nationality, purpose and duration of stay in Dubai.

The transit visa is offered for durations of 96 hours. This visa is mainly used by passengers in transit at Dubai airport who like to explore Dubai enroute to other destinations.

The visit visa is available for visitors planning to stay in Dubai for longer than 14 days. Visit visas are available for durations of 30 days, 60 days and 90 days, as single entry and multiple entries.

The multiple entry mission-based visa is issued only to corporates who receive visitors frequently. The mission visa carries a validity of six months for a stay of up to 30 days at a time.

The business investor visa is issued to investors who run businesses in Dubai. A local partner with a 51 per cent share in the business is a mandatory requirement for this kind of visa.

The student visa is available for full-time college-level students enrolled in listed colleges and universities in Dubai.

Visas for parents, parents-in-law and siblings can be arranged as well as per the guidelines set by the residency department.

Domestic housemaid visas can be arranged provided the sponsor meets the required criteria.

Consular and Legal Assistance

Most expatriates make it a point to register themselves at their country's embassy or consulate as part of their settling down process in Dubai. This is highly recommended as this your link between your base country and Dubai.

This can include cases of being held by the police. Contact your country's embassy or consulate in case you are involved in any disputes in Dubai. Generally as long as you stay within the legal parameters of the law you will be involved with the local authorities. In a situation whereby you are held by the police, a representative of the embassy or consulate is normally allowed to visit you and liaise with your relatives. The consulate representative cannot pay for legal advice or lawyer fees. Do not expect your embassy or consulate to be able to bail you out. Embassies and consulates do not get involved in disputes between companies and employees.

Situations that demand immediate intervention from the consulates are addressed accordingly. Consulates do get involved where cases of domestic helpers and human trafficking are involved. The consulates get involved for sending such victims back home to safety. Other kinds of emergencies can include medical care or political problems during which the consulates take the lead to take care of their nationals' safety.

Liquor Permit

As Dubai is a Muslim city, non-Muslim expatriates who wish to purchase and consume alcohol are issued a liquor permit. Requirements to get a liquor permit include being a legal resident of Dubai, a non-Muslim over 21 years of age and with a salary of more than AED 3,000 (US$ 816) per month.

ACCOMODATION

Many new comers in the city are surprised when they see how well developed, well connected and well maintained and modern the city of Dubai has been developed while they expect camels to be walking around in the desert. If you are planning to live in Dubai for any time period over a month, it is better to rent a space. There is a wide range of apartments and villas available in Dubai, both within and outside enclosed compounds.

Various types of housing options are available in Dubai, from studios to multi-room apartments, to family homes to mansions. Take your pick based on your budget. Your budget may also determine the location. The world's real estate mantra – Location, Location, Location – applies in Dubai too. The location of your new home will be determined by your culture, your way of life, your children's schools, activities of the family, your meal preferences, if you prefer a market area or a quiet side of the city.

Expatriates can buy properties in the classified "freehold and leasehold" areas of Dubai. Dubai's real estate market which was originally only driven by nationals was opened to expatriates in 2002 when His Highness Sheik Mohammed bin Rashid Al Maktoum allowed expatiates to purchase property in Dubai. Following the announcement, there was a massive rush from local residents and foreign investors all eyeing to own a piece or more of Dubai's real estate.

This resulted in a roller coaster ride for the Dubai real estate market, with prices shooting up as much as 70 per cent in some freehold areas. This was a new business trend for Dubai. However, the world economic crash in 2008 affected the Dubai real estate market as well. The fast paced sales and purchases came to a slow down bringing down the value of projects by over 60 per cent, forcing investors to flee the country, developers to slow down or cancel construction of projects and home buyers in mortgage debt for the value of property that had fallen drastically.

Since its inception in 1960, Dubai Land Department (DLD) has handled all matters of legalisation for sales and purchases of land. DLD also approves, organises and documents real estate trading operations in Dubai.

Since its inception in 2005, RERA (Real Estate Regularity Authority) is a regulatory agency that aims to regulate real estate companies, agents and related professionals working in Dubai.

The Bur Dubai, Karama, Oud Metha, Satwa areas house a heavy concentration of the Asian sub-continental community. Many Westerners prefer living across the creek in the newer areas of Dubai like Marina, The Springs, The Meadows, JBR, JLT, Downtown and Business Bay. Some other newer communities in the South of Dubai are Jumeirah Village Circle, Sports City and DIP with several new options available for outright purchase or rentals. If there are constraints in rental budgets, housing options are also available in the neighbouring Northern Emirates of Sharjah and Ajman for those who do not mind spending time in the traffic which is the tradeoff for the low rent.

How To Find a Home In Dubai

The accommodation trend in Dubai is mostly rental. From the time the UAE was formed in 1971 to 2004, foreigners have not been allowed to own property. Hence, all the expatriates that arrive in Dubai had no option but to stay in rented accommodation. In 2004, Dubai opened the property market allowing expatriates to invest and buy property in Dubai. Dubai offers a large range of property both to rent and to buy. Furnished or unfurnished, studio to mansions, these are all available to suit a range of budgets.

Furnished villas or apartments come as agreed in the rental contract. Simple furnishings include kitchen appliances and gadgets. Fully furnished premises include all furniture and appliances.

Finding a Rental Property

Dubai has a comfortable inventory of over 250,000 units that can be rented. The process of renting accommodation in Dubai is simple and straightforward. Most corporates have a list of agents and if that is not available, all details are available on the Internet. Agents are available on short notice to show suitable options. Other ways to find your rental accommodation could be from newspapers or by physically walking around the location. You may find the agent's number on the property for rental.

Once the desired accommodation has been identified, the agent draws up the rental contract at their office. Payment for rent is generally made with postdated cheques. Before finalising the deal, parties need to settle and know:

- Rent per annum. Properties are normally rented on a yearly basis.
- Payment terms. Rent is normally paid by postdated

cheques. A low rent can potentially be negotiated on lesser number of cheques.

- Tenure of tenancy: it is usual practice for rental contracts to be drawn for a period of 12 months. Some landlords accept a lower rent for a longer tenure of tenancy.
- Termination: in case of any possibility of leaving the country on short notice, pay careful attention to the termination clause of the contract. Negotiate how many months of rent need to be paid if the yearly contract is breached.
- The wear and tear clause in the rental contract, to avoid any unnecessary surprises upon vacating. Most landlords expect to receive the property in the same condition as when they leased it out.
- Most rental contracts do not allow for the premises to be shared by any more than the number of persons agreed on in the contract.
- Anti-social behaviour such as disturbance of neighbours or too much noise is not well tolerated in some neighbourhoods.

Rental Costs in Dubai

Rental costs vary enormously for villas of different sizes, some with swimming pools, others without, and between old and new apartment blocks, in good and bad locations. Rents in Dubai vary as per location to size. The easiest way to divide the city of Dubai as Old Dubai or North Dubai and New Dubai called South Dubai. Areas included in Old Dubai are Bur Dubai, Karama, Deira, Oud Metha, Al Ghusais, Al Nahda, Satwa to name a few. Areas of South Dubai include Jumeirah Beach Residence, Dubai Marina, Jumeirah Lake

Towers, Tecom, Barsha, Dubai Investment Park, Dubai World Central, Jumeirah Village Circle, Jumeirah Village Triangle, Sports City, and Arabian Ranches.

The North of Dubai is as vibrant, active and modern as the South. If you want to see the historic and cultural side of Dubai, this is all in the North. 1 bedroom apartments can be rented within the range of AED 70,000-100,000; 2 bedroom apartments can be rented anywhere from AED 80,000-140,000; 3 bedroom apartments from AED 150,000-250,000.

There are not many villas in this part of Dubai, where there's a mix of retail, commercial and residential properties. The South of Dubai includes more recent construction and hence, rents are comparatively higher than in the North. Rents for 1 bedroom apartments range from AED 90,000-110,000; 2 bedroom apartments are rented for AED 110,000-150,000; 3 bedroom apartments from AED 150,000-270,000.

Factors to note when signing your tenancy contract:

- Electricity consumption: one of the major costs of renting property in Dubai is the electricity bill since there is heavy dependence on air conditioning which increases even more in summer. In the annual rental contracts, some landlords tend to include chiller fees in the yearly contract if the property is part of a big complex. The Dubai Electricity and Water Authority (DEWA) issues the monthly bills for electricity and water.

- Cooking gas: some properties have pipe gas lines structured in them with a communal gas tank, with gas costs included in the rent. In some other cases, the tenant is required to get gas bottles.

- Housekeeping services that include cleaning, laundry

and linen changing are part of some serviced apartments and come at an extra cost. Check the facilities and the liabilities on the tenant in such a contract.

Buying a Freehold Property in Dubai

The freehold market was opened in 2004, allowing foreigners to buy property in Dubai. The definition of freehold means ownership of property and freedom to use as preferred by the owner. The Dubai Land Department (DLD) registers and issues title deeds for the freehold properties.

Secure the services of a RERA registered freehold property agent if you plan to purchase property in Dubai. The agent can be of great help, since he will be well versed with the local laws and regulations, and crucially, keeps abreast of any changes in the laws.

Dubai has advanced infrastructure in place, making it an ideal real estate investment destination. Doing your personal research on the neighbourhood, prices, amenities and connectivity will be of great help in finalising the property. In the long term, the Dubai property market is expected to remain positive and offer great rental yield. As a young real estate market, Dubai has resale, off plan and brand new ready properties on sale.

You can find listings for properties in leading newspapers like Gulf News and Khaleej Times. There are plenty of websites where properties for sale and rent are listed. Talking to the agent will offer great insight into the market. Have your list of questions ready. Agents normally speak most international languages including English, Arabic, Hindi and French. There is a standard 2 per cent fee that has to be paid to agents once the purchase is finalised.

Earthquake Resistance

Dubai lies on the Western Coastal Fault Line, in a region that experiences low-to-medium levels of seismic activity. Whenever neighboring Iran experience any earthquakes, slight tremors are felt in Dubai similar to the one in November 2005 when an earthquake measuring 5.9 on the Richter Scale was felt by Dubai residents, causing widespread alarm. Dubai Municipality has stringent building regulations, ensuring all buildings are designed to withstand the forces of earthquakes.

YOUR FAMILY

The first few days: Your first few days may be very likely spent in a hotel. You and your spouse will likely be taken for a medical blood test to test for HIV negativity and Hepatitis B. In certain cases, chest x-rays may be taken too. Your company's public relations officer will help you in this. Once your visa has been stamped, a local identification card called "Emirates ID" will be issued to you and all members of your family.

Take your time to explore the city, the lanes and the communities to decide which one you will call your home. If you are craving your local and authentic cuisine, you can be sure to find it in Dubai.

What to ship in

Your inbound shipping container should have only personal effects that you absolutely would not like to lose. Like that guitar or the favourite pair of shoes, the books or the kids' memoirs. You will easily find a large variety of furniture for your new home in some of the famous home furnishing stores in Dubai, such as IKEA, Homes Center and Homes R Us.

PETS

As more and more foreigners settled down to make home in Dubai, they are accompanied by the very important members of their family – their pets. The local culture does not quite grasp the concept of pets. Dogs are considered impure and black dogs are considered particularly evil, which is the reason expatriates get confused in cases when their pets are hurt or abused. New expatriate communities are trying to advocate for walking tracks for pets. This is necessary due to the hot summer temperatures, long working hours of their owners and lack of free moving spaces. Dogs, cats and rabbits under four months of age cannot be brought into Dubai. All pets must arrive into Dubai as Manifested Cargo; i.e., pets cannot be brought in as accompanied baggage or in-hand or in-cabin luggage. Some breeds are not allowed into Dubai. These include Japanese Tosa Inu, Wolves or

Dogs cross breeds, Argentinian Mastiff, Pit Bull Terriers and American Staffordshire Terriers.

Most expatriates in Dubai live in apartments which are not ideal for pets that need ample space to move around. Pets are not allowed in parks, hotels or malls. Although kennels are available for taking care of pets in the absence of their masters, these are not very economical. Expatriates also face challenges for someone to take care of their pets when they travel for a few days for work or on holiday. It is illegal to let your pet walk unleashed in public. An import permit is issued to allow shipping of pets to Dubai.

BANKING AND MONEY MATTERS

Dubai has several banks of various scales in Dubai. Regional, local and international banks all operate in Dubai, regulated and overseen by the Dubai Central Bank.

Banking facilities in Dubai are comparable to the rest of the world. Most banks offer all modern banking facilities like net banking, debit and credit cards, cheque books, a variety of loans for cars, personal and corporate loans and house mortgages. Signed cheques are a sensitive issue in Dubai. An un-honoured cheque is considered a crime in Dubai. Be sure to always have sufficient funds in your account whenever you issue a cheque.

Banking transactions are closely monitored by the banks. Any suspicious transactions are assessed for their credibility and involve considerable investigation. Everyone who works or has a business in Dubai needs a bank account. You need to have a residence visa before you can open an account. Most banks now require applicants to produce their Emirates ID before opening the bank account.

When it comes to investments, your bank will be able to advice you on investment options available with them. Many banks have tie ups with banks in other countries to provide the convenience of banking with banks in your home country.

Several international insurance companies have offices in Dubai providing loans for car insurance, life insurance, medical insurance and household insurance, among other products. Several expatriates who initiate insurance

policies in Dubai buy internationally covered policies that can be continued in their home countries after they leave Dubai.

Islamic Banking

An alternate yet vibrant way of banking in Dubai is Islamic banking. This type of banking is offered to both Muslims and non-Muslims. The practice of calculating or benefiting from interest or usury is forbidden in Islam and Islamic banking involves the centralisation of funds within a bank. Any business financed by Islamic banking is on a profit-sharing basis and not on an interest-earning basis. For example, funds from Islamic banks are invested into infrastructure projects, which produce returns. These returns are shared out in proportion to input.

Banking for Expatriates

Employers offer most expatriates the options of opening their standard current or savings accounts in international banks. International banks operating in Dubai include HSBC, Barclays, Standard Chartered, Citibank providing retail banking services at reasonable rates. The banks compete locally to offer customers the best rates and terms on their products. Most banks in Dubai offer online banking at international levels. Few banks offer drive-in automated teller machines and banking services after business hours. Don't be surprised if your banking requests take longer than normal time. It is the way of business in the region. Banks in Dubai operate from 8:00 am to 2:00 pm from Saturday to Thursday and are closed on Fridays. Banks in Dubai are closed during public holidays announced by the government. There are several foreign exchange and money transfer retail outlets in the local markets and shopping malls. Money exchanges are also available at all airport terminals and operate 24 hours.

The formalities involved in opening a bank account in Dubai are quite stringent and involve a considerable amount of paperwork. It is mandatory to have a residence visa, which demonstrates your right to be in the country. As already stated elsewhere, you also require a No Objection Certificate (NOC) from your employer. The employer's letter needs to stipulate your salary, to show the amount that will regularly be paid into the bank. Some banks will ask to see your tenancy agreement to establish your residential address, and most will ask for a photocopy of your passport. You should take copies of all these documents, as well as identity photographs.

Current Accounts

Most expatriates keep sufficient cash in their current account. Residents use cash only where cards are not accepted. Most retails outlets in Dubai accept debit and credit cards. All utilities providers like DEWA (for Electricity), Etisalat and Du (for Telephone services) and RTA (for transport services) accept payments using debit and credit cards.

Both local and international banks offer all kinds of standard banking services including credit card payments, cheque clearances, standing orders and direct debits. Cheque books are issued with standard information (i.e., the name of the bank, the branch, your name(s), the date, etc.), and the layout is similar to any international cheque.

Banks accept cheques written in either English or Arabic. Arabic is written from right to left. Bank statements and correspondence can be provided in either language (the application form has a column for preferred language of communication). The business language of the region is English and banking is efficiently carried out in English.

Be careful not to overdraw any amount more than available in your bank account unless you have authorisation from the bank. Some banks honour the cheque if the shortfall is small and advise the customer. The amount is then deducted automatically once the account receives funds. However, if the overdraw is a high amount, the cheque is not honoured by the bank. Banks with good customer service call the customer and give a few

Arabic names tend to be similar, be careful when writing the name of the bearer of the cheque in English. You are not entitled to reimbursement for a "misdirected" cheque if you have been careless and inaccurate when writing it.

hours of time to credit the shortfall of funds in to the account to enable honouring of the cheque.

Savings and Deposit Accounts

You can open a savings or deposit account with any retail bank in Dubai. There are no specific savings banks such as thrifts or savings and loan associations (like in the USA) or building societies or "mutual companies" (like in the UK). Although savings accounts offer lower interest rates than deposit accounts, they have the advantage of easy withdrawal at any time. In many banks, you can open savings accounts designed for major foreign currencies, predominantly the US dollar and British pound. Most expatriates, however, wish to export the majority of their income to accounts outside the region.

Penalties

A bounced or cheque not honoured is considered a criminal offence in Dubai. In cases of larger amounts, the courts get involved and harsh fines and punishments can be levied on the defaulter. Cases of financial abuse are not uncommon and the banks protect their interests carefully, with the support of the judicial system to safeguard themselves against defaulters.

It's important to understand that, in the case of serious financial difficulties, expatriates are unlikely to receive much in the way of sympathy and understanding, since their services in the country are viewed as expendable. In cases of criminal financial actions, penalties are likely to be harsh and might involve confinement for indeterminate periods while the judicial process takes its tortuous course, especially in the more conservative states.

Never issue a cheque without the necessary funds in your account as this is a serious criminal offence and the police will be notified at the discretion of the bank (or creditor) concerned.

For utility bills, direct debits can be arranged with your bank to cover regular payments, but make sure that you check your statements to ensure that these instructions are being carried out. Alternatively, you can pay utility bills in cash at any bank, irrespective of whether you have an account there.

Foreign issued cheques in major international currencies can be drawn into your local account. Following the process of clearance, the amount is remitted into the local account promptly. You might be credited with the amount straight away, but some banks wait for clearance, which can be a lengthy process. If such payments are expected to a regular feature, it is advised to let your bank know so they can advise a less time-consuming way to receive the funds into your account.

Debit and Credit Cards

ATM machines in Dubai accept both locally issued and internationally issued debit and credit cards. Both local and international banks issue debit and credit cards for their customers, which can be used at any branch of the same bank and, by arrangement, at other banks.

Debit cards can be used up to the amount available in the account and usually have a cash usage or withdrawal limit. For example, some local banks restrict daily withdrawal amounts of AED 5,000 or AED 10,000. ATM machines are easily available at the malls, at the banks, shopping centres, at supermarkets, hypermarkets, at cinema halls and other retails and residential districts. Most banks own technologically-advanced teller machines that provide account balances and mini-statements printouts. Most ATMs accept a substantial number of both regional and international cards, invariably illustrated on the machines themselves, although there's usually a fee for using ATMs operated by banks other than your own. Most machines provide instructions and information in Arabic and English.

In case you lose your card into the machine, make sure you are able to call your bank to block your card and call the bank whose ATM machine you were using.

Credit and Charge Cards

A credit card provides access to funds on credit up to a particular limit, upon which an interest is charged, depending on the particular conditions of repayment.

A charge card offers a similar facility but restricts the credit period (usually to a month). Visa and MasterCard are the most widely accepted credit cards worldwide and are the most commonly issued by banks in Dubai. The presence of the Visa or MasterCard name on an unrecognized Arab bank card is important when travelling to other regions. Charge cards such as those issued by American Express and Diners Club are also available in the Gulf and are fairly widely accepted, although less so than the major credit cards, mainly because of the higher commission charged to the supplier of the goods or services.

Most banks in Dubai offer the credit cards for free and with several frills to encourage users to use

Be alert with using different ATM machines. With some machines you must remove your cash quickly or the cash goes back into the machine.

the credit cards for their expenses. If any, the maximum annual fee on a credit card is AED 200 with fees rising for gold cards, which provide higher levels of credit. Many banks in Dubai have tie ups with the major retailers and offers a retailer specialized card with additional benefits, such as travel insurance or life insurance when the card is being used for travel arrangements. Others offer a points system that increases with the amount of purchases, the points being redeemed for consumer goods, travel discounts, etc.

When making purchases in the Middle East, haggling is invariably expected. But the production of a credit or charge card will wipe out any beneficial terms that you might have negotiated. In fact, there might actually be a surcharge if you want to pay with a credit or charge card, particularly if you're buying from a small trader.

You can of course use a foreign credit card in the Gulf and you might benefit from delayed charging, but not if you withdraw cash, for which charging starts immediately. You might, however, find it more convenient to receive your bills in local currency and pay from local funds, rather than be subject to fluctuating currency conversion rates. The western practice of major department stores issuing their own credit cards is uncommon in Dubai, largely because of the cash culture that still prevails in the region.

All credit and charge cards allow you to access cash from ATMs and you might gain some advantage from the rate of exchange as compared to tourist or commercial rates, although you're likely to incur a charge for a cash transaction. There are also occasions when a credit card isn't only useful but a necessity, for example when renting a car or booking into a hotel.

If your card is lost or stolen, make sure that you report it immediately by telephone to the issuing company or bank and confirm it in writing or in person. It's important to keep the telephone number of the card company on hand for speedy notification. Your liability is usually limited until you report the loss.

Cash and Travellers Cheques

Although most places in Dubai accept debit and credit cards, there are still some places where payment is taken only by cash. Generally, being outside your home country, the easiest way to access cash is to withdraw from ATMs easily found at several public places. Most ATMs that display the Visa and MasterCard logos allow for withdrawal to be made. However, there are some charges which will vary from country to country. Tourists in Dubai can easily exchange foreign exchange for local currency. Use one of the exchanges in the city to get a better exchange rate. The currency exchange rates are generally competitive, but commission rates tend to differ if currency is exchanged at airport or hotels. Most hotels tend to charge a higher commission for currency exchange. Local exchanges handle all major foreign currencies, but for obscure currencies it is better to make prior arrangements.

However, some people are apprehensive about using their debit or credit cards in foreign countries and prefer to use travellers cheques when travelling. Travellers cheques are an easier, safer and more convenient way to travel compared to carrying cash. However, at certain times and in some places it can be difficult to cash travellers cheques. Shops and restaurants, for example, don't readily accept travellers cheques. Apart from banks and currency exchange centres, most hotels also change travellers cheques, but at much poorer rates of exchange. Banks charge a small commission for exchanging travellers cheques and the exchange rate is invariably better than that offered for the conversion of banknotes. Proof of identity (e.g. passport or ID card) is required.

It's unlikely that you will be able to purchase travellers cheques in UAE dirhams, and, as the currency is tied to the US dollar, you should use US dollar cheques (or cash) in order to avoid possible exchange fluctuations.

Athough it's convenient, avoid changing travellers cheques to any currency other than that of the country you are visiting. For example, if you're travelling to Oman first and then Dubai, resist the temptation to change your money in Oman to meet your needs in Dubai. If you do, you're likely to find that the exchange process takes two steps: if you're buying Saudi riyals in Bahrain, for example, your euros or dollars are first converted to Bahraini dinars and then from Bahraini dinars to Saudi riyals. Although the Bahraini and Saudi Arabia currencies are linked, the foreign exchange will charge a commission on each transaction (in this case two transactions).

Foreign and Offshore Banking

Traditionally, the super-rich used offshore banking to stash their millions and save tax payment in their home countries.

The general rule of thumb among a majority of expatriates is to maintain three months of their salary in the current account and wire the balance to the offshore account. Many couples also maintain offshore accounts to stay clear of the Sharia law that applies to all expatriates (irrespective of their religion) in case one of the partners passes away in any circumstance. Anyone wanting a joint account with his wife or a business partner would be well advised to hold that account outside of Sharia law, which generally means an offshore account. Among the most popular destinations for banks are Isle of Man, Jersey, Guernsey and different cities in Switzerland, including Zurich and Geneva.

Most local and international banks operating in Dubai offer offshore banking accounts. Citibank, Barclays and HSBC are some of these. Expatriates who move countries more frequently prefer to maintain their cash and savings in multiple currencies. Instead of maintaining current accounts in several countries, it is much simpler to maintain one offshore account through which funds can be managed efficiently. There are more than 300 offshore accounts for UAE residents to choose from. Expatriates use only their offshore accounts for most banking transactions including getting their salary transferred, managing loans, house mortgages, credit cards and life insurance.

An offshore bank account may be advantageous if you want to earn interest while keeping funds reasonably fluid in the short- to mid-term. An offshore account can be used as a central source from which to send funds to other locations, including an account in your home country. Other attractions are that money can be deposited (and maintained) in a wide range of currencies, customers are usually guaranteed anonymity, there are no double taxation agreements, no withholding tax is payable and interest is paid tax-free.

Sharia Law in Banking

Many expatriates in the Gulf countries are not very well aware that the legal framework followed in their host country is generally that of Sharia law and this can impact their accounts and funds.

According to Sharia law, account and assets can be frozen upon death. The wife does not get access to the husband's account immediately. Should death occur while the person is residing in Dubai, Sharia law is applied to any assets that are held in the UAE. Death of males and females are handled differently. In case of the demise of the wife, all her assets revert to her husband, but if the husband dies (even if it a jointly held account), the account is frozen immediately. Apart from bank accounts, any other assets like businesses or cars registered under the name of the husband are impounded until the court decides on the beneficiary of the man's assets. This process takes time, stretching from a few weeks to several months. In some cases the rulings are issued for the bulk of assets to be passed to the closest male relative of the deceased man (his father, brother or son). Although the female partner faces a disadvantage at the legal front when it comes to assets and banking, there are chances a clearly-defined will, duly notarised by the courts is taken into consideration. Hence, wives of expatriate men should maintain their own cash flow accounts or have easy access to a joint offshore account. In several societies, the surviving widow and children become the responsibility of his immediate surviving family, but this may not necessarily be the case as societies have now moved to nuclear families. Therefore, in cases of emergency, offshore accounts which are not impacted by Sharia law can be of great benefit.

COSTS OF LIVING

As in any major metropolitan city, the costs of living in Dubai have been steadily rising over the last few years as the city adds consumer services and facilities to its infrastructure. Nonetheless, Dubai remains one of the easiest and most convenient places to relocate in the region. You may hear from several people that living in Dubai is getting more and more expensive gradually. This is because Dubai is heavily investing in electricity, water, roads, medical infrastructure, innovation, education, digital marketing and constantly striving on improving the standard of living in this city. All these projects require huge investment injections which the government inputs on a majority basis. However, with the strain on oil prices, governments are re-strategising their balance sheets, revenues and expenditures. Dubai plans to introduce 5 per cent VAT from 2018.

- house rent including power, water and cooking gas
- school fees
- holidays
- food and transport
- others, such as shipping and entertainment costs

Most families easily pay over 40 per cent of their income in rental costs. In case of school going children, school fees take up another big chunk of the income.

Food Prices

Locally produced food items are available at low prices, however imported groceries can seem high priced compared to how much you would pay for the same product back home. Although you will find every known food item, drink and household product in Dubai, the price variation should be expected. The price of liquor where the sale is permitted is higher; however the availability is always assured. Household white good and electronic goods, such as televisions, music systems, mobile phones and tablets, photography equipment and computer hardware and software are generally reasonably priced here in Dubai. If you buy internationally recognised branded foods and household goods, this can take away a further part of the monthly budget as most products are imported into the country. For fresh food items, there are usually plenty of cheaper locally and regionally produced alternatives that are of excellent quality. Shopping for clothes, shoes, watches and bags can be slightly expensive compared to their Western counterparts.

Utilities

Electricity, water and gas are subsidized for the local Emiratis. Expatriates are expected at full rates. Electricity, water and gas are billed as per the meter based on consumption of individual households. In addition to this bottled water and cooking gas come at additional costs. Expect your electricity bills to increase in summer when air conditioning is required mostly throughout the days and nights. The electricity and water bill is issued by DEWA (Dubai Electricity and Water Authority) and has per unit costs of consumption of electricity, water and housing fees included in the bill. Utilities are therefore cheaper than in most countries. Billed statements are expected to be paid within one month failing which supplies can be cut off and reconnection charges apply. Electricity bills tend to hike up in summer due to excessive

A rough budget of expenses:

- House rent for a two bedroom apartment costs between AED 100,000 and AED 150,000 per annum. Additionally, expect to pay AED 1,500-2000 towards electricity, water and gas utilities.

- Schooling: High school costs about AED 40,000 to 80,000 (fees can be up to AED 110,000) per annum, while primary school costs between AED 20,000 to 35,000 per child at international schools following the American, British or European curriculum taught by teachers from the Western countries.

- Maid services can cost around AED 3,000 per month.

- Transportation costs can marked at AED 2,000 per month (fuel at AED 600 per month and AED 3,000 for car insurance)

- Utilities: Depending on the size of your home electricity and water can cost between AED 1,200 and AED 5,000 and a full time maid costs at least AED 12,000 per annum.

- Car rental: cars can be leased for AED 1,500 per month which would mean an annual cost of AED 18,000.

- Telephone: local calls are free, local calls from mobile phones are 15-30 fils per minute. Mobile data and Internet flat rate costs approximately AED 400 per month.

air conditioning requirements compared to lower bills in winter months. Newcomers sometimes make the expensive mistake of keeping their air-conditioning on even when they leave their homes pushing up their bills significantly. A better alternative is turn on the air conditioning immediately on returning home with the cooling system not taking too long to bring the indoor temperature down. The bill is expected to be paid every month in order to continue receiving the services. In case of any problems with electricity and power, the number to call is 997.

TELECOMMUNICATIONS

Telecommunications in the United Arab Emirates is under the control and supervision of the Telecommunications Regulatory Authority (TRA). Etisalat and Du are the official telephone operators of Dubai. A visit to the Etisalat office will be of help in the few first days to apply for your home land lines, mobile and Internet connections. It is suggested to carry your passport copies with your stamped visa page and your Emirates ID when you go to apply for telecom services. Etisalat provides all kinds of business and personal telecommunications services. Du is another telecoms service provider established in 2006 to offer mobile services across the UAE and Internet and TV services to some free zone areas.

Visit the Etisalat or Du offices to get your phone lines. To get a mobile line you will need to show a salary certificate from your employer. A telephone line is usually installed within one or two working days. Mobile numbers get immediate connection within a couple of hours.

The best and cheapest way for tourists travelling to Dubai is to get a pre-paid SIM card (Wasel). The prepaid cards can be purchased online, at Etisalat or Du offices or at retail outlets. To buy a pre-paid card, the passport copy is required along with the fees to startup the SIM card. Service is activated within one hour.

EDUCATION

Dubai is experiencing a rapid expansion in the education sector and with top universities from all over the world setting up campuses, the emirate is gearing up as a preferred educational destination for students in the region and abroad.

Dubai currently has 265,000 students of 183 different nationalities studying at 173 schools and about 26,100 students enrolled at over 26 universities in Dubai. Private schools in Dubai offer education in seventeen different curricula. Some of the more popular ones are the International Baccalaureate, and the American, British and Indian CBSE. Schools are staffed by teachers from India, Australia, the UK and US. Schools are well equipped in their infrastructure and offer rigorous academic programmes with well-rounded extra-curricular experiences.

Places at entrance levels are more difficult to secure than at mid or high secondary as there is a higher percentage of younger families migrating to Dubai. Thus, there is a higher demand for the 4 to 7 years age group. Parents are advised to apply at more than one school to successfully secure a place. Admission in schools is granted to children over four years of age at the time of admission.

Your one point of contact for schools in Dubai is the KHDA (Knowledge and Human Development Authority). KHDA runs an annual assessment of all schools across Dubai every year, placing schools within bands ranging from unacceptable to acceptable, good and outstanding, based on a grid of internationally standardised crucial criteria. KHDA aims at improving the levels of schools and other institutes in Dubai by bringing them to internationally recognised standards. Pay a visit to KHDA's office at Dubai Academic City to get a personal consultation for your preferred school. The KHDA website provides a complete list of educational institutions in Dubai and their KHDA ratings and reports.

Two factors that impact school timings in Dubai are the summer temperatures and reduced working hours during Ramadan. Schools generally operate between 7:45 am to 3:00 pm. There are several co-education schools in Dubai. Education is free for locals. Expatriates are charged fees for private schools, which are usually allowed to raise fees by 20 per cent every three years.

University Education

Dubai International Academic City (DIAC) is the world's largest free zone dedicated to higher education. DIAC is the premier destination for higher education in the region, located on a fully-appointed 18 million sqft campus offering a large selection of multi-tiered International Branch Campuses (IBC's), from 10 different nationalities and is host to a community of over 24,000 students from 145 nationalities who have access to over 400 higher education programmes.

Some of the programme options available at DIAC include Fashion, IT, Technology, Chemical and Mechanical Engineering, Accounting and Finance, Business, Supply Chain, Architecture, Interior Design, Media and Communications and Biotechnology. For more information, see www.diacedu.ae.

International Students in Dubai

International students are increasingly choosing to study at universities in Dubai. Dubai is evolving as the most attractive educational hub both in the region and internationally, as it offers many advantages that international students look for in their host country like safe, clean and good quality food, easy connectivity to most international cities, international exposure and most importantly, a non-racist and culturally diverse environment. Most of the universities use English as the medium of instruction. Dubai also offers varied attractions for students, including sports and recreation, shopping and dining.

Dubai also offers a wide spectrum of vocational training options. Established in 2003, Dubai Knowledge Village is dedicated to the fields of Vocational Training, Human Resource Management, and Executive Search and Professional Development.

Foreign universities operating in Dubai include:

- Manipal University
- Heriot-Watt University
- Amity University
- Middlesex University
- University of Wollongong
- Hult International Business School
- Rochester Institute of Technology
- BITS Pilani
- Institute of Management Technology
- American University of Dubai

MOVING AROUND

Transport in Dubai is controlled by the RTA (Roads and Transport Authority), the government body that covers the various government transport services from metros, buses and trams to marine transport services. RTA strives to reduce traffic congestion in the city, making Dubai roads free of emissions.

The Nol card is required for the Dubai Metro, Dubai Bus, Water Bus, Dubai Tram and also works for paying some taxis. The Nol card is free for disabled people and national senior citizens, while students benefit from 50 per cent off Nol card rates.

The most popular transport option is the Dubai Metro, which operates throughout the major malls and landmarks of Dubai. Two common fines include eating and sleeping in the Metro. The Dubai Metro currently runs on two lines – the Red line and Green line. The red line began on 9 September 2009 while the green line commenced operations in 2011. The Dubai Metro will continue to expand the lines to cover further areas of Dubai.

Dubai Bus which runs across the city is also a comfortable way to get around the city. All Dubai Buses are air-conditioned and so are the bus shelters. Very soon the bus shelters will be able to offer Wi-Fi for passengers. The Dubai Bus service aims to feed passengers into the Dubai Metro.

In addition, there is the Palm Monorail that connects the Palm Jumeirah to the mainland. The Palm Monorail is more popular among the tourists. The Dubai Tram that opened in 2014 runs along the Al Sufouh road and Jumeirah Beach road from Mall of the Emirates to Dubai Marina. The Dubai Tram moves at an average speed of 12 kmh. Water taxis, *abras*, are used to cross the creek between Bur Dubai and Deira.

If you plan to use any public transport services in Dubai, it is advisable to get a Nol card. Nol cards are easily available at all Metro stations.

Driving in Dubai

If you would like to drive around the city, you will require either an international driving license or a regular driver's license

A Dubai Metro carriage. All stations and trains are air-conditioned, so this is a very popular mode of transport.

issued by RTA. To get a driver's license, you must be over 18 years of age and you will need to sign up with any of the local driving schools. On being issued a learner's permit, you will be required to take 40 classes before taking the test for a driver's license. The test involves a theory exam and a road test. The theory test involves knowing road signals, completing a questionnaire and identifying the right driving conditions. The road test is focused on real driving skills and the driver's ability to handle the car according to the assessor's instructions.

Nationals of GCC countries or the following countries can exchange their license and get a Dubai driving license issued upon passing an eye test that is available at several hospitals, clinics and authorised opticians: Australia, Austria, Bahrain, Belgium, Canada, Denmark, Finland, France, Germany, Greece, Ireland, Italy, Japan, South Korea, Kuwait, Netherlands, New Zealand, Norway, Oman, Poland, Portugal, Qatar, Romania, Saudi Arabia, South Africa, Spain, Sweden, Switzerland, Turkey, the United Kingdom and the United States. Persons holding a driving license from Greece, Canada, Cyprus, Poland, Turkey, Japan and South Korea will need their license translated from their consulates. If you are not planning on driving a private vehicle, but a rental car, you will not need a temporary driver's license, as an international driving permit will be sufficient.

Both locals and expatriates in Dubai are passionate about their cars and their number plates. Many consider that their social status is judged by their car's number plate. The number plate business here is huge and there are many businesses and agents who specialise in procuring sought-after number plates. In general, the fewer the digits on your number plate, the more important you are considered. Three-digit plates and anything lower can easily run into six-digit figures in UAE dirhams. Sequenced or repetitive plates such as 123 or 1313 can also significantly increase the price of a number plate. The UAE currently holds the record for the world's five most expensive number plates ever auctioned – in 2008, plate number 1 was auctioned for AED 52 million (US$ 14.5 million. RTA holds regular online auctions where selected number plates are auctioned for sale to the highest bidder.

Motoring Life

With just under 700,000 registered vehicles in Dubai, and with more than a million cars on Dubai's roads each day, the car is the most popular method of transport in the emirate.

The road network around Dubai consists of between one and five lanes of traffic in each direction. Blue, green or brown signposts are written in both English and Arabic and, as the network is constantly expanding, road works are everywhere. Although the GPS system works well around the city, inner roads have unofficial names and it's the norm for people to navigate by landmarks and location maps.

Dune Bashing – Driving in the Desert

You will be amazed at the size of the cars you will see on the roads in Dubai. While these 4x4s look classy on the highways, you will see their real power unleashed in the sand dunes. Dune by dune, one by one, desert driving is best learnt here in Dubai. The deserts aren't too far from the city. In less than an hour, you can reach the desert to test yourself in raw nature.

If you are a mountain driver, take the route to Jebel Hafeet or Jabal Al Jais mountains. The views from the top are mesmerising. You can even join one of the many off-roading clubs of Dubai. Many of these clubs are informal and formed by expatriates who share a passion for driving in nature.

Many expatriates cannot get enough of the adrenaline rush of driving in the desert. The whole experience of jumping up and down the different heights

Take an experienced driver along to guide you through the dunes. Most driving schools offer a one-day desert driving course to train you in driving in the dunes. One you feel you are ready, explore the many wadis that will challenge even the best driver's skills.

of the sand dunes is a favourite pastime, especially in the winter months where the dune bashing days lead into bonfire evenings with barbeque aromas filling the desert air. Many driving schools offer a one-day desert driving course with a trained instructor.

The adventure of driving in the desert includes navigating through bumps, rocks and shrubs and rocks. Driving slowly is the key in the desert as hitting a bump at high speed can damage the suspension and hitting a rock at high speed can damage tyres. Try to avoid the shrubs and bushes as they can puncture tyres.

Congestion

Traffic congestion remains a huge problem in Dubai. So much so that the emirate's first toll gate system, Salik (meaning "clear" in Arabic), opened in July 2007. Stretching from Garhoud Bridge to the junction of Mall of the Emirates along Sheikh Zayed Road, motorists have to purchase a pre-paid card and affix a machine-readable sticker to their windscreen. As they drive along the route, they're charged AED 4 each time they pass an electronic toll, up to AED 24 a day.

Dangerous Driving

Despite good tarmac roads and well-maintained vehicles, Dubai's roads are some of the most hazardous. According to a 2006 UN report, the UAE's roads are the third most dangerous in the world, with 20 deaths per 100,000 people. Saudi Arabia is the most dangerous with 23 deaths per 100,000 people, and Oman second with 21 deaths per 100,000 people.

Each year, the number of deaths and serious injuries from road accidents increases, despite police efforts, which include rewarding motorists who drive safely, employing mobile radar devices and increasing traffic patrols. Statistics from the Dubai Traffic Authority indicate that 97 per cent of accidents in the emirate were caused by male drivers. With the winter rain comes even more chaos than usual. One wet February morning saw 500 accidents of varying seriousness reported before 9.00am, the result of motorists failing to adapt to the wet road conditions, speeding and not leaving enough distance from the vehicle in front. By the end of two days of rain, figures showed there had been an accident every two minutes during that period. The police cite the main causes of death on the roads as reckless driving, speeding, colliding with stationary vehicles, ramming into the right side of vehicles, head-on collisions and jumping red lights.

Blood Money

Blood money is a penalty paid to the family of the deceased in case of loss of life and also damage caused to a person's body part in a car accident. Blood money or "Diya" amount is fixed at AED 200,000 (US$54,700) and has to be paid in case the victim was not accountable for any error in the accident. Where blood money is an option, the judge assesses the extent of damage, be it moral or material. In case the blood money cannot be arranged, the driver has to serve a jail term decided by the judge.

Car Crime

Car theft is very unusual in Dubai, with very low crime rate in terms of car theft or broken cars. The efforts of the Dubai police and regular patrolling help to keep crime at bay. Motorists are however urged not to keep their car engines running, leave the car unattended or keep any valuables inside the car.

Mobile While Mobile

Motorists caught using their mobile phones while driving could face jail in a new initiative launched by the police. Currently, a police officer's power is limited to dispensing advice.

In another initiative, the police have launched a new SMS alert service, with motorists alerted on their mobile phones when they commit an offence.

Car Rental

Hiring a car in Dubai is generally considered simple. Car hire rates are generally inclusive of registration, servicing and insurance. To hire a car in Dubai, the driver needs to be at least twenty five years old, with at least two years' driving experience and a valid international driving license from an approved country. Due to the nature of the visitors in Dubai, many car rental companies will quote prices per month; shorter times are of course available. Customer service and care is important in Dubai and most car rental companies, owing to the competitive market, are reliable and attentive. It is important, to be aware of how much things cost before you arrive, to prevent being ripped off.

Shop around on comparison websites for the best deals, in order to be prepared upon arrival. Renting while in Dubai, however, can be far cheaper, as you have the opportunity of negotiating with the company, which is advisable. For example, the average cost of renting a car, in Dubai, is AED 58 to AED 143 per day. Depending on how long you plan to stay for, it is advisable to book a car for a short time upon arrival in order to have a hassle free journey from the airport and if you plan to stay for longer than a few days, shop around in order to receive the best deal possible.

Tourists with a valid international driving license from an approved country are eligible to drive in Dubai. Drivers over the age of eighteen and holding valid insurance documents for the hired vehicle are allowed to drive in Dubai. Most international car hire companies have operations in Dubai. Vehicles are driven on the right side of the road in Dubai. Children below the age of 13 are prohibited to sit in the passenger seat and younger children until the age of eight are required to sit on a booster seat. The Tram is a new addition to the Public Transport and drivers are expected to educate themselves with the fines associated with driving near the Tram. Some driving schools offer classes specialised classes like desert driving and Tram theory. Road signs and speed limits are clearly marked on the roads. Speed limits are set for minor roads, intercity roads and highways.

The Fine System in Dubai

Drivers are expected to follow RTA guidelines at all times. There are over 200 types of penalties that can be issued by RTA in case of driving faults. To keep improving the driving standards in Dubai, the Dubai police has developed a "Black Point System" wherein every driving penalty includes a certain number of black points. Driving whilst under the influence of alcohol incurs the greatest number of points (24) and penalties: your car will be confiscated and court proceedings will take place. If any alcohol has been consumed, taking a taxi is advised.

Some driving penalties lead to the license being revoked or the car impounded. At reaching 24 points, the driving license is revoked for a period of one year. There is an option to transfer the black points to another driver.

Some of the major fines include:

- Beating a red light
- Driving without a seat belt
- Driving under the influence of alcohol or drugs or similar substances
- Causing any physical harm to anyone on the roads including injuries
- Driving in the way of the tram

The Driving Style

Being an international city with residents coming from over

over two hundred countries around the world, every driver in Dubai has his own style of driving. For newcomers, driving in Dubai can be both enjoyable as well as intimating. It takes time before drivers are able to find their own style of driving around the inner roads, the highways and the streets of Dubai.

It is a good idea to be more careful and drive slowly nearing Iftar time in Ramadan. People observing the fast try to reach home early.

RTA has invested in sophisticated speed controlling systems in Dubai to keep both drivers and passengers safe at all times. Speed cameras called "Radars" are increasingly installed at most roads to record not just speeding but other offences committed by drivers. In this way, RTA has been very successful in reducing the number of road incidents and casualties year on year.

HEALTH CARE

Public hospitals in Dubai are managed by the DHA (Dubai Health Authority) who ensure the services, facilities and the quality of the hospitals and clinics are well-kept at all times.

Dubai offers world-class health care and medical facilities. Both public and private hospitals in Dubai cater to local Emiratis and expatriates. While the locals are provided free health care at the public hospitals, expatriates choose to visit private hospitals as they are mostly covered by medical insurance. English is widely spoken at hospitals and clinics. There are sufficient numbers of clinics and hospitals to serve the population. Some specialisations have longer appointment waiting times than others. Some private hospitals in Dubai have five star facilities like TVs in the room, air-conditioning and mosque or prayer rooms, libraries and on-call meals.

Specialisations offered at the hospital include: ENT, family medicine, dentistry, breast surgery, bariatric surgeries, ophthalmology, radiology, sports surgery, dermatology, gynecology and obstetrics, cardiology, neurology, neonatology, pediatric care, pulmonology and psychiatry. Most of the private hospitals have out-patients departments, trauma and emergency units. Some of the well-known public hospitals are Rashid Hospital, Latifa Hospital (gynecology & obstetrics and pediatric care) and Dubai Hospital. However, the most widely referred to is the trauma unit at the Rashid hospital especially for construction-related or road accidents. Among the private hospitals are Mediclinic, City hospitals, Welcare hospital, American Hospital, Neuro-Spinal hospital, Saudi German hospital.

There are pharmacies in every area that operate 24 hours a day. Be careful before you bring along any medicines from your home country in your baggage to Dubai. Several medicines are only allowed in with a prescription. Dubai has strict laws and controls on medications like sleeping pills and

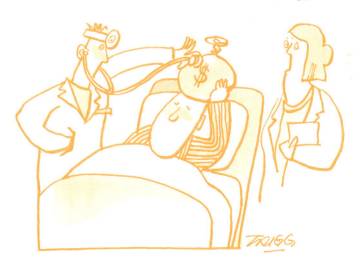

anti-depressants; these are prohibited from being sold over the counter, and sometimes illegal. These are only available if you have your doctor's prescription.

Dubai has mandatory insurance requirements for all its residents and tourists.

Doctors and specialists practicing in Dubai come from all over the world. There are some local doctors and medical staff practicing as well, but a large number of medical staff come to Dubai trained from their home countries.

All employers in Dubai provide medical insurance for their employees. The insurance package is negotiated between the insurance company and the employer. Some even cover dental insurance. Expatriates commonly visit hospitals and clinics for common colds and coughs and dust-related problems. The summer months bring several dehydrated patients to the hospitals with the mercury rising to 50°C. Most residents avoid being outdoors in summer and activities are restricted to the indoors.

Most doctors and nurses speak basic Arabic and fluent English. All practicing doctors are endorsed either by the Ministry of Health or, if attached to military establishments, by the Ministry of the Interior. Doctors in the latter category are also available to the general public under certain circumstances. Many doctors and nursing staff practicing in Dubai come from Europe, the USA, Egypt, India and Pakistan, and their qualifications are verified by the Ministries before they're allowed to practice in Dubai.

Health and Dental Insurance

The Dubai Health Authority issued a law in 2015 requiring all residents, locals and expatriates to have medical insurance. This includes children, elder dependents, visiting relatives as well as domestic helpers. Locals are provided health insurance by the Government. Expatriates are provided health insurance by their employers. While it is mandatory for employers to provide medical insurance to their employees, most employers provide medical insurance to the employee's family as well. There are several international insurance companies specialising in private health insurance in Dubai who offer insurance covers to suit various budgets and medical requirements. Policies can be easily compared between them.

REGISTERING BIRTHS

The hospital provides the documents required to get a birth certificate. The application should be made within one month of birth of the baby with the baby's name on it. The birth certificate is issued by the Ministry of Health. Once the birth certificate has been issued, make sure the baby's visa has been applied within four months of the birth. The visa has to be applied at the General Directorate of Residency and Foreign affairs, Department of Naturalization and Immigration.

GETTING MARRIED

As long as both the bride and groom is Muslim, getting married in Dubai is simple. However, with a high number of expatriates from several countries and religions residing in Dubai and deciding to tie the knot in Dubai, the best option is contact their individual embassies to enquire about the process. The required paper work takes about a month to be arranged. The legally permissible age for marriage is 18 years for both men and women. Once married, if marriage certificate is issued in English, it is required to be translated into Arabic by an official translator to make it a valid document to be used for official purposes.

Arabic Marriages

Traditionally, in Muslim families, marriages are legal once puberty is reached; however, with the increase in awareness and education levels, this is rapidly changing, especially over the last ten years.

Traditional local Emirati marriages were made within the tribe, to ensure women of the tribe stayed within and were kept protected; related families would intermarry. This also strengthened the ties of the tribesmen. Tribal marriages were also favoured as the families would know each other well compared to giving away the girl to an unknown tribe. Unlike their western counterparts, local weddings in the past meant the man would only see his bride after the marriage formalities were completed on paper and they were legally wedded.

There are three main elements to an Arab wedding. First, the groom must discuss and agree the dowry (mahr) with the bride's father. This might include gold, jewellery and clothing, usually of considerable value. After the dowry settlement comes the actual marriage contract, which is conducted by a legal or religious representative. The bride is asked in the absence of the prospective groom if she agrees to the marriage and this question is then put to the groom. After agreement, the groom joins hands with his future father-in-law and, with two witnesses present, the marriage becomes official. However, there's another stage before the couple actually meet as man and wife: the wedding party.

Wedding Celebrations

Since the culture is basically Islamic, in local weddings, men and women have totally separate wedding celebrations. The wedding celebrations are carried out separately in different halls on the same night. Prior to the actual wedding evening, the bride is pampered with traditional oils and perfumes. This "ladies only night" or Laylat Al Henna is celebrated on a grand scale with women only – there is singing and dancing and feasting and the hands and feet of the bride are elaborately decorated with henna. On the day of the wedding, the female celebration of the wedding is quite sober on the outside, but once the female guests step inside, it is a completely different world to be experienced. The female guests who go in modestly dressed in their Abayas and Sheilas remove them once they are in all-female company. Women tend to dress over the top for the weddings, even as guests, with elaborate dresses, gowns, makeup, jewellery and perfume.

The wedding is celebrated with music, dance and ample food (no alcohol is served).

Older women in the family tend to be even more warm and receptive of guests. When the celebrations are almost ending, it is a custom for the groom, his direct male family, and the bride's direct male family members to enter the women's wedding hall. This part of the wedding is like the male members of the family "dragging the groom" to his new wife. Finally, the new groom and bride will sit side by side socially for the first time. Local weddings are rapidly raising the bar: some weddings are now held at seven star hotels instead of family homes, endless feasts are laid and the crème de la crème of the social circle are invited to the wedding. Hotels, on their part, offer the best service, massive catering menus, fairy tale stage decor and lighting, top-notch wedding favours and music to create a truly memorable experience for all.

If you are invited at a local wedding, it is considered an insult if you refuse their dining hospitality. Locals are very social and warm and enjoy socialising with guests at weddings.

Mass Weddings

In order to mitigate the burdens on young citizens looking to get married, the Marriage Fund organises mass weddings to support and encourage Emiratis to marry within the community by facilitating the required means.

The Marriage Fund has held over 44,000 weddings since 1992, reducing both the number of marriages between Emiratis and non-nationals and of unmarried Emirati women. The Marriage Fund helps young couples to a great extent to reduce the wedding costs and start life without the burdens of debt.

Marriage for Expatriates

Dubai has a clearly defined process for expatriates who wish to tie the knot locally. To begin with, both the bride and groom should be holders of valid UAE residence visas. Apart from set documents, witnesses are required at the wedding. Many expatriate couples prefer to marry at their holy place of worship like a temple, gurudwara, church or at their local Embassy or Consulate.

For Muslim Expatriate Weddings

In case the bride and groom are Muslims and not UAE citizens, both the bride and groom are required to hold UAE residence visas. Applications are to be made at the Marriage Section of the Dubai Court by the bride's father or guardian or his attorney and two Muslim witnesses. In case the bride is Muslim, and her father is not, she needs a No Objection letter from her embassy (or consulate) in Arabic (or translated into Arabic and attested by the Ministry of Justice) and attested by the Ministry of Foreign Affairs. The court then issues a marriage license.

For Christian Couples

For a Christian couple who wishes to get married in a church, the latter requires a certificate of No Impediment to Marriage issued by your embassy before conducting the ceremony. A marriage certificate is issued by the church in English, which needs to be translated to Arabic and notarised.

For Hindu Couples

Wedding ceremonies where both bride and groom are of Hindu decent are conducted by the priest at Hindu temples, although the wedding alone is not considered legally recognised. Prior to the wedding, the couple is required to apply for the marriage notification to be published in a local newspaper. If no objection is received within 30 days, the couple will be given a date for the solemnisation of the marriage. The temple requires a pre-approval from the consulate to solemnise the marriage. Both bride and groom have to hold valid UAE residence visas.

Authenticate any marriage certificate for its validity by getting it notarised, attested by the Ministry of Justice, the Ministry of Foreign Affairs and then your embassy (or consulate).

Divorce

Marriage is Islam is governed by the guidelines of Sharia Law, which lays a lot of emphasis on the importance of marriage, encouraging tolerance, patience and respect in a marriage. It has been designed specifically to make it difficult for couples to divorce. Like couples anywhere around the world, reasons for divorce remain broadly the same: lack of trust, financial strain on either partner to continue in the marriage, lack of modesty by partner, emotional or physical abuse, mental or physical deficiency, or cruelty.

Any couple seeking to settle a divorce in Dubai needs to first get their documentation right, without which the courts do not look into the case. This involves the legal attestation and translation of the marriage contract. Once the documents are arranged, the case needs to be filed at the Moral and Family Guidance Section of the Dubai Courts. It is here where family counsellors hold sessions with both parties, attempt to reconcile any difference and encourage the couple to give their alliance one more chance. The appointed counsellors try to get the couple to agree on spending some more time together to reconsider the marriage. Failing this, the case is then forwarded to The Court of First Instance, i.e., the Personal Status Court. In Islam, divorce is considered legal if a man announces "I divorce you" three times. This is called *talaq* (that is, the formula of repudiation). The female's right to seek a divorce is called *khula*. The divorced female is granted alimony by the husband.

THE LEGAL SYSTEM
The Islamic Legal System
In general, Gulf states operate as largely patriarchal societies, headed and administered by ruling families, whose aim is to maintain the status quo while moving towards increased democracy (although in many cases the authorities seem to follow the old adage: "If it ain't broke, don't fix it.").

Legal Sources
The Islamic system of law, known as *Sharia* (or *Shari'a* or *Shariah*), derives from several sources: the Holy Koran (*Qu'ran*) Islam's Sacred Book, and the Sunnah, a verbally transmitted summa of Muhammad's teachings. The Holy Koran, being the word of God (Allah), is the principal source. The Sunnah comprises the accepted deeds and statements of the Prophet Mohammed, accepted by the whole Islamic world (the *Ummah*). It also involves the *Ijma*, a consensus among religious scholars (the *ulema*) regarding solutions to matters not specifically covered in either the Koran or the Sunnah. In difficult cases, where there's no information to provide the basis for a clear decision, "analogous consideration" (*qiyas*) is applied in conjunction with the three other sources.

Trials

In Sharia law, as in other legal systems, a person is presumed innocent until proven guilty. The plaintiff and defendant are equal before the law – i.e., in a court of law – and it's incumbent upon the former to provide proof of guilt. This involves producing two or four eyewitnesses, depending on the seriousness of the crime. If a plaintiff isn't able to produce eyewitnesses, he can insist on the defendant swearing an oath as to his innocence. If the defendant refuses to take this oath, he's judged to be guilty, as perjurers suffer hellfire and eternal damnation according to Muslim belief. Jews and Christians swear a different oath, but it has equal validity. A judge (*qadi*) presides over the court and can put questions to all parties at will. There are no juries and often no lawyers to present the case for their clients. There are systems of appeal, which can be used in cases of serious crime and punishment.

Compensation

According to ancient law, the payment of "blood money" (*diya*) for injury or death can be requested by the victim's family as compensation. The amount of blood money required varies between the states (it's most likely to be exacted in Kuwait, Saudi Arabia and the UAE) and according to the circumstances of the death and to the extent of the hardship that the death will cause. For example, the death of a father of 12 would attract a larger payment than that of a child. A local Muslim's life will be assessed for a larger financial benefit than people of other religions, faiths or nationalities.

Under Islamic law, the crimes that carry defined penalties are murder, apostasy (rejection or desertion of Islam), adultery, fornication, homosexuality and theft. Interpretations of the law and punishments vary from state to state. Lesser offences might include debt, usury, alcohol and drug abuse, and use of pornography.

How Courts Are Composed

The legal system in Dubai is based on Sharia, civil and criminal law, implemented by the Federal Judiciary, which comprises courts of first instance and supreme courts. The Supreme Council of Rulers, the highest ruling body in the UAE, appoints the five members representing the Federal Supreme Court, who preside over matters concerning constitutional law and rule on cases affecting disputes between any of the emirates and the Federation as a whole. Local government plays an important part in legislation within each emirate.

Sharia Law for Expatriates

As an expatriate, you're subject, of course, to the laws of the country you're in. If you're thought to have broken a law, you're taken under arrest to a police station, questioned and instructed to make a statement. Up to this point, it's highly unlikely that you will be allowed access to outside help, either legal or consular. If the offence is deemed serious enough to warrant your detention, you might have to wait some time before your case comes up. You will be allowed legal representation, but everything will be conducted in Arabic. Your statement will be translated into Arabic, and it's important to insist that an appropriate official, e.g. a member of staff from your consulate, checks the accuracy of the translation and the content of anything you're required to sign. If no one is available to do this, you should refuse to sign, or sign with an endorsement to the effect that you don't have a clear understanding of the document.

Online Behaviour

The TRA (Telecommunications Regulatory Authority) cautions people who are active in the online world to be careful not to share their passwords with others, post vulgar or inappropriate photographs, make funny comments about religion, post photos without their consent and threaten others.

Social Security

Dubai does not have obligatory state or employer-contribution insurance schemes. A small population and respectably high gross domestic product allow Dubai to fund the welfare of their people without needing to impose many financial obligations upon them. This also means that the governments avoid the high costs of administering such schemes. Nationals are automatically provided with extensive state help, including medical care, sickness and maternity cover, child care, pensions, unemployment benefit and in some instances, housing and disability benefits.

Foreign workers have access to medical facilities. In fact, Dubai is beginning to pressurise companies to provide medical insurance for their employees to ease pressure on state healthcare for expatriates, and recommend private medical insurance for most foreigners.

New Expatriate Toolkit

Below is a toolkit to help any new expatriate settle down in Dubai.

- Get the visas and Emirates ID for yourself and your family in order. This is an important first step since without a valid visa and Emirates ID, many other things cannot be arranged.

- In order for your visa to be processed, you will need to undergo a medical test. This can be arranged by the company's public relations officer and can be completed within four days.

- Emirates ID application happens along with visa application but takes time to be issued. Tip: Keep the Emirates ID application number handy and keep following up with the Emirates ID department (www.id.gov.ae).

- Get No Objection Certificate (mentioning your name, nationality, salary and length of service) from your employer for:

  1. Opening Bank Account
  2. Obtaining Liquor Permit
  3. Driving License application
  4. Telephone landline application
  5. Mobile and data line application
  6. Importing your pet

- Once No Objection Certificates have been issued by your employers, you can open your bank account and transfer funds into it.

- Apply for your driving license so you can move around easily in the city.

- Apply for your landline and mobile lines so you are connected to the online world.

- Visit several schools to finalise the most suitable school for your children. Many schools have waiting lists. The school will require mobile numbers and visa copies before confirming admission.

- Obtain your liquor permit (only for non-Muslims).

- Process the import of your pet.

CHAPTER 6

THE FOOD OF THE WORLD COMES HERE

CUISINES AND TASTES

Dining out – in the pursuit of new cuisines and tastes – is an informal national sport of Dubai. It is easy to be spoilt for choice. Wish for it and you are sure to find here. Dubai is very proud of the fantastic assortment of international restaurants that have made their success stories in Dubai. Excellent Arabic cuisine, including Jordanian, Syrian and Lebanese, are all to be had in the city alongside Indian, Pakistani, Thai, Korean, Chinese and just about any world cuisine. Dubai is home to over 8,000 cafes, cafeterias, standalone restaurants

An Italian restaurant at The Walk at JBR, one of the thousands of international food options available in the city.

and fine dining restaurants catering to all budgets and tastes. Many establishments are even more authentic and of better quality than those back home in their native countries. As Dubai is a Muslim city, alcohol is not served in cafes and restaurants, and available only inside hotel restaurants. Here is also one of the few places you'll find a camel burger – high in protein, with less than half the fat contained in a traditional beef burger.

According to a recent survey, 35 per cent of the residents dine out at least two to three times during the work week and the number increases to 50 per cent on weekends. The latest apps available on the fingertips of the smartphone users are helpful and convenient, as diners can place orders for just two or for a whole party with just a touch on the smartphone, making it easy to book restaurant tables and order takeaway and packed meals, anytime and anywhere. Most people in the office order in lunches on weekdays. Younger couples do not find it feasible and financially viable to cook for one or two people. Dining out and ordering in work out to be better options.

Apart from catering to its growing cosmopolitan expatriate population, Dubai eateries also serve the millions of holidaymakers who reach Dubai on a daily basis, international students who come to Dubai for studies and the thousands of single men – making it a whole lot of mouths to feed.

Heading Upmarket

Dubai boasts of over 20 celebrity chef restaurants. Gary Rhodes, Pierre Gagnaire, Atal Kocchar, Sanjeev Kapoor, Luke Thomas, Richard Sandoval, Vineet Bhatia, Giorgio Locatelli, Jamie Oliver, Marco Pierre White, Vannick Alleno, Wolfgang Puck, Vikas Khanna, Simon Rimmer, Antonio Carluccio,

Silvena Rowe and Jason Atherton are some of the celebrity chefs who run signature restaurants in Dubai, each offering dishes that form a story waiting to unfold, a gastronomical journey to be explored and a discovery of tastes. At many of these restaurants, prior table reservations are required and many have a dress code. Over the top quality cuisine equated with the highest prices are a status symbol and a reflection of the high flying lifestyles of the rich and famous locals and expatriates, who don't mind paying rack rates for ambiance and the chance to spot a few celebrities while dining.

A 10 per cent service charge and 10 per cent municipality fee is added at many tourist establishments, particularly hotels, although you are free to add more if the service was particularly impressive. If the charge is not included, 10 or 15 per cent is about average. Although tipping is not mandatory, the tipping culture in Dubai is varied since the expatriates come from different countries around the world with different practices.

Budget Options

Some of the budget areas to get a decent meal are Karama, Oud Metha and Meena Bazar and 2nd of December street,

The main protein that is cooked and wrapped in bread for a *shawarma*.

where mid-range to budget restaurants offer food from countries including India, Iran, Pakistan, Thailand, China and Nepal. Quality checks are carried out regularly at all food outlets in Dubai. Most restaurants in the city are open until 11:00 pm on weekdays and midnight on weekends. Well-known names are Rangoli (Gujrati), Karachi Darbar and Ravi's (Pakistani), Pars (Iranian), Lemon Grass (Thai).

High Tea

Dubai is home to some of the most luxurious, tempting and mesmerising high tea spots. The British pastime of high tea has a whole new take in Dubai. To the uninitiated, high tea may be a confusing term. Essentially an early evening meal between 3:00 pm and 6:00 pm, high tea consists of cold meats, eggs and/or fish, cakes and sandwiches. Some of the best high tea lounges in Dubai are Atmosphere lounge at Burj Khalifa, Al Fayrooz lounge at Al Qasr, Madinat Jumeirah, Fortnum and Mason, Rhodes W1, Sky Tea at Burj Al Arab, Crossroads at Raffles Dubai, The Lobby Lounge at Ritz Carlton, The Farm at Al Barari and the Lotus Lounge at Anantara The Palm Dubai. Make prior reservations as most of these locations get full quickly for high tea.

THE LOCAL CUISINE

Most people think that *hummus*, *moutabel* and *toubuleh* make up Emirati cuisine. Many are unaware that Emiratis have their own cuisine.

A favourite local drink across Arabic homes and offices is the Arabic coffee called *qahwa*, paired with dates. This is a standard offering to be found throughout the day. The traditional Emirati cuisine is high on protein with a variety of meat, seafood, pulses and vegetables grown locally.

Some of the local dishes include *harees*, *fireed*, *ma'louba*, *frsee'ah*, *margooga*, *machbous*, *jisheid*, and *mishwy*. Emirati main courses are cooked like stews with not much spice. Fragrant spices like turmeric, thyme, cardamom, sesame, rosemary are used for flavouring.

A unique Emirati breakfast includes date syrup, breads like *khameer* and *chebab*, eggs and cheese. *Khaboos* is freshly baked bread eaten with cheese, kebabs and fish. A favourite dessert dish is *luqeymat*, deep fried balls of pancake batter rolled in sesame seeds and then dipped in date honey; and *khabeesa*, bread crumbs blended with sugar, cardamom, and saffron.

Like most Arabs, no meal ends without black tea which is called *sulamani* by local and expatriates alike. Pork and alcohol are not part of Emirati cuisine.

The Hunter Gatherer

Locally produced fresh vegetables are available easily in Dubai. Local supermarkets are the best place to go – reasonably-priced and well stocked with fresh food to easily make your own meals. Shopping for your own food won't be too difficult in Dubai. For Asians, the major supermarket chains of Choithrams, Al Maya Lals and Lulu offer all the staples. The Al Adil chain has also gone into offering a larger variety of Asian spices and packed foodstuff. Along with fresh fruit and vegetables and standard groceries, Geant, Park and Shop, Carrefour, Spinneys and Waitrose cater to the daily needs of international tastebuds. There are aisles dedicated to different cuisines in

Bring your sharpest bargaining skills. Your negotiation skills will definitely come to use at this market.

these supermarkets. For a more traditional experience, head to Bur Dubai souq where you can buy nuts, spices and grains at a bargain.

Ras Al Khor Market

Once you have got your driving license and car, take a drive to the Dubai Fruit and Vegetable market at Ras Al Khor. Tip: use the GPS in your car or mobile to reach this market. It is advised not to venture to this market by metro or bus. The next best option is to go by taxi. The market is an open market located in Ras Al Khor Industrial Area 3.

This market is more ideal for large families or for those whose consumption of fresh fruits and vegetables is substantial enough to buy in bulk. A visit to this market is a food shopper's dream

Bottled local honey.

as they can walk around little alleys and rows of fruit and vegetables vendors. The only disadvantage of this market

Arayes, meat stuffed into pita bread and baked for a savoury treat.

Luqeymat, little balls of batter, deep-fried and dipped in sugar syrup.

is the extreme heat in summer. Shopping outdoors can be especially difficult in this market as shoppers end up with several big bags of purchases that need to be carried back to the car and to the house.

BEING A GUEST

A good guest always acknowledges the invitation from his host. Taking a box of dates, chocolates or flowers will make your host feel good. Local men greet each other by touching noses. Your host will greet you saying "Ahlan Wa Sahlan" which means welcome. As a foreigner, a handshake will be fine. Do not offer to shake hands with the women of the house, though a smile is always welcome. Between the women, a warm hug and shaking hands is permitted.

Shoes are not allowed in the house; visitors are expected to take their shoes off before entering the house. Emiratis are sensitive to shoes being pointed towards them and take offence. It is good manners to use your right hand when you are handed some food or drinks. Do say "Shukran" which means "Thank You".

Arabic homes generally have two living areas. The area where the men sit to chat and eat is called the *majlis*. Women of the house have their own *majlis*. Don't be surprised and certainly don't ask if you don't see the females of the house around. If you are going with your wife, your wife may be escorted to the female *majlis*. You can be assured she will be well taken care of.

The *majlis* area is kept clean at all times to receive guests and to offer them *oud* (Arabic scents), coffee and date. You may be expected to remove your footwear before entering the *majlis*. So make sure your socks are not stinky or torn! Inside the *majlis*, you may be seated on the floor. Sitting flat on your feet is advised, avoid pointing toes or soles to anyone sitting across from you. Refreshments are offered at the *majlis*. Use your right hand to eat unless you are absolutely left-handed. Show respect if an elder or senior person walks into the *majlis*. This will surely impress your host as locals hold family values with high regard.

Very likely an invitation is offered for dinner. Don't expect an invite before 9:00 pm. Arabs like to relax after a long day with a late dinner. If you have been invited for dinner, expect

Don't show up at a local family's house unannounced.

to enjoy a lazy evening with food, coffee and conversation. Your local host will be keen to listen to your views and about your lifestyle and culture. Avoid topics like religion, politics or anything that is too personal in nature, unless you are very close friends. Arabs like to share incense (*oud*) with guests. Be careful when you appreciate a rich possession, as your host may end up gifting this to you.

INVITING YOUR FRIENDS HOME

If you make friends with the locals and would like to invite them over to your home, be mindful that women may prefer to sit in another room and not mix with other men freely.

Do compliment them on the smell of oud that will fill your home when they enter. A useful phrase on this occasion would be "Ahlan Wa Sahlan" which means "You are welcome".

Once you make friends with the locals, they will bring a fresh perspective of their ways of life and the way they look at the world. They are as curious as you are about cultures, traditions, family units and homes. A lot of the younger generation Emiratis are well travelled and may even surprise you with their knowledge.

Don't expect your Emirati friends to dance with you to music or be game for a session of karaoke. Modesty is part of the Arabic culture.

And just as across all cultures, food binds all. A lavish spread will be appreciated by your guest.

What's New On the Food Scene?

Just like other parts of the world, the food truck concept is new to Dubai. The best mobile kitchens have arrived in Dubai finally, serving burgers, fries, milkshakes, cookies, juices, coffee or Mexican nachos. The trucks are stationed at specified locations.

CHAPTER 7

ENJOYING DUBAI

> ❝Dubai is an unpolished gem polishing itself very quickly. You could look at it as a CD compilation – the best of London, Sydney, Miami, and Las Vegas.❞

— Robert Gogel, CEO of Integreon, Inc.

A TOP TOURIST DESTINATION

Dubai is all set on being a top tourist destination. However long you plan to stay in Dubai, whether a one-day stopover, a short family beach holiday or a month-long summer holiday, Dubai will keep you thrilled, amused, entertained and excited. Discover Dubai at your own budget with a large variety of accommodation options available from budget hotels to furnished apartments to luxurious high-end hotels. Draw up your own itinerary to cover the culture and history of Dubai, shop for jewellery or simply enjoy the yearlong sunshine at the clean beaches.

Dubai Marina, an artificial canal city offering hundreds of residential, dining and retail options. The construction involved directing the flow of water from the Persian Gulf into Dubai Marina.

Tourist Attractions

- Visit the local market (*souq*). There is one in Bur Dubai and another across the creek in Deira. Take the metro or jump into a taxi to get there. Try taking a ride in a small boat (*abra*) that local commuters use to cross the creek. You may get chit chatting with local residents who enjoy talking to tourists.
- Visit the Gold Souq and be impressed by an endless glittering collection of gold, diamonds and precious stones.
- Visit the Dubai Museum and Al Fahidi Fort to see Dubai's past and the origins of the Arabs.
- Go on a desert safari, an attraction which includes dune bashing, driving through the desert dunes, being entertained with belly dancing, camel rides, getting *henna* on your hands and feet, and finishing off with a grand Arabic buffet.
- Visit Dubai's pride. Buy tickets to "At the Top", the viewing deck at Burj Khalifa. Go close to sunset to admire both the daytime and sundown views of the city.
- There is much more to do including visits to Dubai Mall, Ski Dubai, Wild Wadi Water Park, Dubai Autodrome and the Burj Al Arab.

THE PARTY NEVER STOPS

In one moment you could feel you are in the East and in another, you may feel you are in the West. Dubai has a buzzing, colourful and vibrant nightlife with a lot on offer. From the streets and the pubs and fine dining restaurants to music concerts and the theatre, the party never stops. The clubs are located inside the hotels. Stroll into one of the several seven-star hotels in the middle of the night and feel like the evening's just begun. The city hosts internationally recognised DJs, musicians, bands, artists and singers from around the world. Some of the well-known artists who have performed in Dubai are Katy Perry, Chris Brown, David Guetta, Martin Garrix, Nicky Minaj from the West and Shah Rukh Khan, Salman Khan, Amitabh Bachchan and Akshay Kumar from Bollywood. There are several clubs that have

Ladies Nights on weekdays where ladies can enter free and are offered freebies.

Go-To New Year's Eve Destination

Every 31 December, Dubai becomes the must-go destination for people around the world to experience New Year's Eve. The Burj Al Arab and Burj Khalifa draw millions of visitors to celebrate the year's end. The royal Burj Khalifa becomes the centre of attraction. Visitors and residents alike begin to gather by 2:00 pm to secure the best spot to see the fireworks. Many claim it is a once-in-a-lifetime experience with the lights, the music, the excitement, the fireworks and the ambience around the world's tallest building. Fireworks are coordinated at the strike of midnights to start at Burj Khalifa, Burj Al Arab and Atlantis Dubai.

The Fantasy World of Movies

Several Bollywood premieres have been held in Dubai with stars visiting the city to promote their movies. Bollywood movies like *Happy New Year, Humari Adhoori Kahani* and *Welcome Back* were shot here. Dubai entices even Hollywood. *Mission Impossible*, *Fast and Furious*, *Wall Street* and *Star Wars* were filmed in Dubai. Some of the most visited cinemas in Dubai are Vox Cinemas and Reel Cinemas.

Dubai has been hosting the Dubai International Film Festival (DIFF) since 2004. This is an influential platform for artists, technicians, writers, industry experts and film makers. Visit www.dubaifilmfest.com for more information.

SHOPPING

Name a product or brand and I promise that you can find it in

Dubai. Perhaps due to the intense heat in the UAE in the summer, Dubai has developed some of the world's most glamorous and varied air-conditioned shopping malls. Being tax free, prices are often very competitive.

Among the malls are Dubai Mall, Mall of the Emirates, Wafi Mall, Ibn Bututa Mall, Mercato Mall and Souq Madinat. Dubai is home to the biggest and best malls in the world. The mall culture is very vibrant with every brand opening its doors in the malls. Year on year, retail brands from across the world arrive in Dubai to establish their presence.

Dubai Mall, which spans over 1.1 million sq m (12.1 million sq ft) of retail and entertainment, is the world's most visited shopping and entertainment destination. The mall houses The Gold Souq; The Fashion Avenue; Dubai Aquarium and Underwater Zoo with thousands of aquatic animals; KidZania, SEGA Republic, a 7,060.6 sq m (76,000 sq ft) indoor theme park; the Olympic-sized Dubai Ice rink; and a 22-screen multuplex cinema with a capacity of 2,800 seats. The Dubai Mall also hosts a 155-million year old dinosaur. The Dubai Metro has a stop at Dubai Mall station.

Mall of the Emirates, with 233,467 sq m (2.5 million sq ft) of entertainment and shopping space is home to Ski Dubai – the Middle East's first indoor ski resort and snow park. It also houses Magic Planet for children's leisure; a 14-screen multiplex cinema; the Dubai Community Theatre and Arts Centre (DUCTAC) which seats 500; and more than 90 international dining and cafe options. For the convenience of guests, the mall has two hotels adjoined to the mall, making it the perfect holiday mall for tourists.

Other well-known malls in Dubai are Mercato and Ibn

Battuta Mall offering world-class shopping, dining and entertainment experiences. Malls in Dubai operate from 10:00 am to 10:00 pm with hours extended liberally during public holidays, Dubai Summer Surprises, Dubai Shopping Festival and Ramadan. While prices at the local *souqs* can be bargained over, prices at the malls are fixed, although many stores hold sales very often.

Souqs

Souqs, traditional local markets, offer a dose of the real Dubai and are a must see, especially with winter visitors. Vying for space along narrow streets, the many outlets are noisy and aromatic, and vendors will engage you in conversation, offer you soft drinks, tempt you with offers to buy their spices, rugs, silks and gold, and allow you to sample many of their edible wares.

Just about 15 years ago, locals and residents in Dubai shopped at the *souqs* for groceries, vegetables, fruit and spices. These charming traditional *souqs* can still be found. Take a taxi to the Meena Bazaar in Bur Dubai where you will see the retail outlets in their best glory. If you feel even more adventurous to explore the local markets, try to reach Deira which is a completely different world compared to the malls. Here is where you will see the oldest areas of Dubai doing business. Markets in Deira include the Baniyas market, Naïf Souq and the Gold Souq. Some of the area local markets are in Satwa and Karama.

What many visitors talk about Dubai

Tourists at the local *souq*, a stark contrast to the modern air-conditioned malls in the city.

is the larger than life, tallest, biggest, excessive qualities and extravagance. But Dubai has its own history, own character and there exists a real Dubai which is very different from the post card pictures. Put on your walking shoes with comfortable clothes and take the walk to the Bur Dubai market. Outside your comfort zone perhaps, here is where you will find the real Dubai: traders vying for your attention, lanes and lanes of handicrafts, spices, perfumes and lots more. This walk may end up being the most interesting part of your travel to Dubai. Wander in the small lanes, preferably in the evening when the market is buzzing and you will be able to smell the coffee. You may almost return back mesmerised by the startling difference between the cultural and modern

Ittar or Arabic perfume: non-alcoholic, strong and bold, these fragrances are not for the faint-hearted.

sides of Dubai: the lavish giving way to the cultural; the modern giving way to the traditional; the designer stores giving way to the local standalone stores; franchise food outlets giving way to local bakeries and cafes. If you are a photographer, this is your paradise to capture your best shots. Try hopping on a small boat to cross the creek from Bur Dubai to Deira. The small boat called the *abra* is a traditional

Arabic wooden boat that carries passengers between the sides several times a day. *Abras* are the cheapest way to cross the creek at AED 2 per ride per person. For this fare the *abra* offers an amazing way to watch the real city of Dubai.

Take the taxi to the Gold Souq in Deira. Once there, try to bargain on the marked tags on the gold jewellery, to save yourself some pocket money.

Visiting the Gold Souq

A definite bucket list item for most tourists is to visit Dubai's Deira Gold Souq. All that glitters there is indeed gold: this is Dubai's biggest and richest jewellery market. The Gold Souq has no mall. Expect to walk outdoors around the tiny lanes as you peruse continuous

Stalls at the Gold Souq started with traders from India and Iran opening businesses here. The place has not looked back since, and is today one of the city's most visited tourist spots.

displays of gold jewellery, diamonds, silvers, precious stones, watches, all more than your eyes can select or your mind can choose. The stores at the Gold Souq offer gold in 18, 21, 22 and 24 carats. Gold jewellery in Dubai arrives from designers from around the world – including Bahraini, Indian, Italian and German – if you have a jewellery design in mind, you are sure to find it here.

Deira Spice Souq

The Gold Souq will give you a very good idea of what to

expect in the local markets. Walk into Deira's Spice Souq as the aromas of spices tang in the air. The Spice Souq is located near the Deira Abra station and Gold Souq. Tip: let go of your taxi at Al Ras. Walk through the inner lanes and explore the sights and smells of the local stores. Spices here come from Iran, India and Pakistan. The *souqs* have been there for a long time since development began in the area, and are not dependent on tourists for their business. Local residents come here to buy spices, herbs and grains.

A variety of grains, pulses and nuts, sold by the weight at the Spice Souq.

Bur Dubai Textile Souq

If all that glitters is gold then explore the Bur Dubai Textile Souq to get dazzled even more by colours and more colours as you skim through the endless standalone stores offering fabrics from around the world. Name it and find it here, be it cotton, wool, silk, georgettes, satin or polyester, the stores have it all. The stores stock endless reels of plain printed and textured fabrics. In the same market, you will be able to find tailors who can tailor your latest dress for you complete with a large range of borders, clips, laces, sparkling sequins and buttons. Tailoring services are reasonably priced and tailors provide prompt delivery from a couple of hours to a day. So whether your choose to pick just the fabric and design

A kaleidoscope of colours, fabrics, bits and bobs in Dubai's historic Bur Dubai district.

your own dress or a ready-made dress catches your fancy, the Bur Dubai Souq is an impressive lane for the ones who like to dress up. Do sharpen your bargaining skills in this market and end up with some extra cash left in your pocket. You can pick up a local *shawarma* from a Persian Cafeteria that has been serving fresh *shawarmas* for the last 35 years from the same place in the textile *souq*.

Hardware and Machinery

Ace Hardware is your destination to visit to get all your handyman tools for the house. Ace Hardware has two outlets, one on Sheikh Zayed Road and in Festival City. They stock all household tools like paints, gardening equipment, tools, camping equipment, wall paper, plants among other household tools.

Electronics

You will be able to find electronic and household appliance shops at all malls in Dubai. The electricity supply is similar to UK and Europe: 220 volts. Some of the well-known electronic outlets are Sharif DG, Carrefour Hypermarket, Jacky's Electronics and Jumbo Electronics where you would be able to find all household electronic appliances and white goods for your home. Please keep your receipt in case you would like to exchange your purchase.

Furniture

The world is here in Dubai when you begin exploring furniture for your home and office. The high-end brand Harvey Nichols is located at the Mall of the Emirates and they stock brands like Ralph Lauren, Armani and Missoni. Another recognised brand Bloomingdale's located at Dubai Mall offers all household products that you have on your wish list.

Other furnishing stores around the city include Pottery Barn, Ikea, Homes R Us, The One and Home Center.

Apparel and Accessories

Name it and you will find it in Dubai. Every international brand has a presence in Dubai. From the high-end Louis Vuitton, Dior, Prada and Chanel to H&M, Marks and Spencer, Zara, Gap, Banana Republic and Michael Kors – these are all in Dubai.

Jewellery

When it comes to jewellery, Dubai holds the record to woo every woman's heart. You will be able to find an endless collection of gold, silver, pearls, diamonds, and precious stones in Dubai. From international designers' jewellery brands to local designers, Dubai dazzles and impresses with

Those shopping for jewellery would be thrilled at street after street of jewellers.

jewellery to suit every budget and taste. Gold designs come to Dubai from India, Thailand, Sudan, Bahrain, Russian, Italy and Spain among others. Certified diamonds and solitaires are available very easily. Take a visit the Dubai Gold Souq in Deira or one at Dubai Mall or Bur Dubai to find yourself asking for more.

EXPERIENCING RAMADAN

Ramadan is a holy month for the Muslims during which fasting is observed from sunrise to sunset. It is the ninth month of the Islamic Lunar Calendar and considered to be one of the most important months for Muslims. Fasting during Ramadan is one of five pillars of Islam. If you happen to be in Dubai during Ramadan, this one month will surely change your perspective about the city, its culture and people and perhaps change you too in many ways. All residents, locals and expatriates are expected to follow the guidelines of the culture during Ramadan. The major changes that may impact you directly will be no eating and drinking, dressing modestly and showing patience and consideration to Muslims around you who may be fasting. Greet people saying "Ramadan Kareem" which means "have a peaceful Ramadan".

Dubai makes Ramadan an unforgettably pleasant experience for both the locals and the expatriates. Do try out the Ramadan buffets (deals are all available online to start with) if you haven't been invited for Iftar either by your colleagues or friends or neighbours. Iftar is the time when Muslims break their day long fast with some juice and dates followed by their favourite dishes. You may see the city sleepy during the day and come alive at night after Iftar.

For new expatriates, the first-time experience of Ramadan can differ from one country to another. It is prohibited to eat, drink or smoke in public during Ramadan. Dressing up modestly is a sign of showing respect to Muslims and non-Muslims both around you.

In Dubai, Ramadan is considered a very enriching and fulfilling experience. During Ramadan, there is a sense of compassion, patience, modesty, patience and generosity in the way people deal with each other and generally life inside and outside homes. Friends and family gather more often during Iftar when it is time to break the fast with a large spread to satisfy everyone's tastes. Men and young boys head out for prayers to the nearby mosques while the women pray at home or at the ladies' section at the mosque. Evenings during Ramadan are spent doing special night prayers called "Taraweeh" in Arabic. Many Muslims distribute food at the local mosques and give alms to the labourers and the less fortunate. NGOs and volunteer groups organise several events to distribute food, gifts and daily essentials during Ramadan as it is considered a month of generosity.

FESTIVALS

Islam dominates the way of living in Dubai. The two main festivals of the city are Eid Al-Fitr, which is a festival marking the end of the holy month of Ramadan, and Eid Al-Adha, the festival of sacrifice which marks the end of Haj (the pilgrimage that Muslims make to Makkah in Saudi Arabia at least once in their lifetimes). Prophet's Ascension (Al Isr'a Wal Mairaj) and the Prophet's Birthday (Milad Al Nabi) are other public holidays.

Although not counted as public holidays, Hindu festivals like Holi (colour run and fun) and Diwali (the festival of lights), Easter and Christmas all make their presence felt in the windows, doors and traffic in the city.

In Dubai, Eid Al-Adha normally lasts two to three days and Eid Al-Fitr lasts four or five days. Government offices tend to have a few more holidays compared to the private sector. Islamic holidays are determined by sighting the moon and UAE sets up a moon sighting committee prior to any Eid announcement.

LOCAL FOLKLORE

Traditionally, local Emiratis left home for several months during the pearling season. The leader (called 'Naha'an') on the diving boat (locally called the *dhow*) would lead his team and keep their spirits going with music and song. The Naha'an would start off the singing and the team would join him in the singing in rhythm to inspire each other.

The local Emirati folklore has a strong passion for poetry. A traditional musical instrument is called Oud, an ancient stringed instrument that is the ancestor of the European lute. The Ayyala is a traditional dance performed by the men, and can be seen at the heritage village in Dubai.

> On the home front, the Emirati woman would sing this song as she awaited her beloved to return home safely:
>
> *Neighbour of mine, my adventurous sailor shall return.*
>
> *Neighbour of mine, he shall return from the world of dangers.*
>
> *With perfumes, precious stones, rose-water, and incense he shall return.*
>
> *He shall return, and to see him again will be like seeing the Moon.*

EXPLORING DUBAI

Try joining a group with the Sheikh Mohammed Centre for Cultural Understanding which has been established as a non-profit organisation to showcase Dubai's culture to its visitors and new residents. The concept of "Open Doors. Open Minds" simply means "know about us and tell us about you". A variety of tours include creekside tours, visits to the Mosque, and visits to the traditional Arabic house and the local market (*souq*).

Whether you do it alone or with a group of friends, let the city amuse you, entertain you and amaze you with its architecture, music, attire and lifestyle.

Some Tours To Try

- Dubai City Tour
- Dubai Desert Safari
- Dubai Cruise Dinner
- Dubai Hatta Safari
- Dubai Falconry Safari
- Dubai Camel Polo Tour
- Dubai Hot Air Balloon Tour
- Dubai Fishing Tour
- Dubai Marina Cruise
- Dubai Helicopter Tour
- Dubai Pearling Tours
- Dubai Seaplane Tours

Sightseeing on an open top bus is a good way to see many city sights in an easy, hassle-free way.

Art Galleries Around Dubai

Over the last few years, Dubai has been evolving as the art centre of the Middle East. The contemporary art scene in Dubai is buzzing today with some very sophisticated galleries that have a rich and rare collection of art on display. The website www.artinthecity.com is a good place to find art galleries in the city. Make sure you get the location of any of the galleries right as they tend to be tucked away in the interiors of the city.

Well-known Art Galleries

- The Majlis Gallery founded in 1989 is the oldest art gallery in Dubai and located very close to the old part of Dubai and the museum.
- Cuadro located in Dubai International Financial Center houses works of contemporary art from both local and Western artists.
- Tashkeel supports the local artists of UAE by offering studio facilities, artists' residencies, international fellowships, and exhibitions events and recreational workshops.
- The Empty Quarter, also located in the Dubai International Financial Center, displays high-end photography.
- Jam Jar in Quoz is an art gallery and school for amateurs to try their hands on painting and also for professionals. Jam Jar also holds several art events for both kids and adults.

ACTIVITIES AROUND DUBAI

The world comes to Dubai to celebrate life, food, culture, literature, jazz, art, lights, books, health, boats, movies, bikes and most importantly, to design tomorrow's industries today. Here's a brief list of events around Dubai.

Dubai International Film Festival (DIFF)

Since its inception in 2004, DIFF has gone from strength to strength, helping to develop a thriving film culture within the region, provide greater opportunities for Arab film makers and offer invaluable cultural benefits to the people of Dubai and the UAE.

The DIFF, now in its 13th year, has been included in Condé Nast Traveller magazine's list of the world's top 15 film festivals for the second year running, reaffirming its status as a leading international film festival and a hub for film making in the region. DIFF earned its spot on the magazine's hot list as a platform to discover the best in Arab cinema and an exciting destination to mingle with A-list stars. The list highlights the world's most travel-worthy cinema events with DIFF being named alongside the most prestigious film festivals in the world including Cannes Film Festival, Venice Film Festival, Toronto International Film Festival and Berlin International Film Festival.

Emirates Literature Festival

The Emirates Literature Festival is held in Dubai every year, bringing together the largest collection of authors, writers and thinkers from all over the world. The festival is a bookworm's dream come true. Every year it only gets bigger and better than the previous year. The show is spectacular with bespoke dinners in a fine dining setting along with authors talking about their personal experiences of writing the books. The literature festival also holds reading, writing and film making workshops. In 2015, it welcomed 140 authors along with over 37,000 visitors attending over 200 events arranged as part of the festival. The written collection attracts school children, scholars and thinkers who build life changing friendships during their visit to the events. Many are awestruck to meet their favourite authors and hear them talk about their experiences. The books cover a large variety of languages from English to Arabic to French, and many more.

Dubai Jazz Festival
Making its debut in 2003, The Dubai Jazz Festival is the most awaited jazz festival of the region. The festival runs over a three-day period attracting thousands of music fans from Dubai and other neighbouring countries. The Jazz Festival is held at the Dubai Media City amphitheater for three nights.

Middle East Film and Comic Con 2016
If you thought Dubai can spoil you, wait till you visit the Middle East Film and Comic Con and get charmed. MEFCC is the platform that brings together cartoon characters, comic characters, superheroes, celebrities, musicians and artists from across the world. The MEFCC event is the perfect day out for kids who love to see their favourite comic characters come to life and cannot stop taking pictures with them.

Dubai Holding Vertical Marathon 2016
The Dubai Holding Vertical Marathon has been held for the last four years and is a unique marathon that is carried out at the Jumeirah Emirates Towers. The Vertical Marathon is run up 1,334 stairs, over 265 metres (869.4 ft) climbing 52

floors. Contributions from the Dubai Vertical Marathon are handed over to Al Jalila Foundation to aid in medical research on obesity. Dubai's Vertical Marathon is the 5th highest in the world after Taipei, Hanoi, Beijing and New York.

Rugby Sevens

Opened in 2009, The Sevens Stadium is one of Dubai's leading sports and entertainment venues. The official home of the Emirates Airline Dubai Rugby Sevens, the three day annual rugby extravaganza, the venue has hosted international football, cricket and other rugby events, along with sell-out concerts. Some big names have already performed here, including Rod Stewart, Spandau Ballet, Justin Bieber and One Direction. They've recently added an eighth pitch dedicated to rugby, football, Gaelic football, Aussie rules, American football and even baseball. The facility also boasts four floodlit multi-purpose outdoor courts and three grass cricket ovals, two of which are floodlit. The Sevens Stadium is also available for hire, for events ranging from corporate conferences to private parties. With a stadium capacity of more than 50,000, there's no need to be strict with the guest list. The Sevens is owned and operated by Emirates Airlines, and is on the Al Ain Road, approximately 40 km (24.9 miles) from Dubai.

Dubai Air Show

Debuting in 1986 as Arab Air, Dubai Airshow has evolved as the biggest regional and international magnet for the players in the aerospace industry. The Dubai Airshow brings the most dynamic players of the aviation industry to Dubai showcasing the latest and greatest in military, general and commercial aviation. The order book of The Dubai Airshow 2013 recorded 1,040 exhibitors from 60 countries, totalling US$ 206.1 billion, the largest order in any air show history.

Dubai International Boat Show

Dubai International Boat Show brings the best of marine industry to Dubai covering sailing, watersports and fishing. The show attracts more than 30,000 visitors from over 120 countries who come together to experience luxury and elite super cars, super yachts, marine equipment, leisure crafts, interactive watersport activities, marine supplies and marine services.

Dubai Art Show

Dubai is evolving as an epicentre of new world art. International artists bring the best of their works to Dubai to exhibit at the Dubai Art Show. The show is an ideal platform that provides art lovers in the region the chance to admire works of art from countries including India, Europe, South American and Seoul. The galleries display some of the best work of the artists and are a great tool for bringing the art community together. The Dubai Art Show exchanges paintings ranging from AED 35,000 to AED 365,000 (US$ 1,000 to US$ 10,000), raising the bar of artistic extravagance higher each time. The lineup of works displayed is spread across categories like Islamic art, contemporary art, Modern and classical art. The show is held in partnership with The Abraaj Group and is held at Madinat Jumeirah.

Dubai Canvas Festival

Dubai Canvas is an annual festival with varying artistic themes each year. This time around, Dubai Canvas presents a 3D art festival. Visitors will be able to see a number of optical illusions created by 3D artists brought to Dubai from around the globe by the Dubai Media Office. The event aims to promote Dubai as an artist's dream holiday destination. Attending the event are a variety of art bloggers, media personalities as well as VIP guests.

Dubai Food Festival

Dubai is a city that brings the cuisines of the world to the doorsteps of its people. Undoubtedly, The Dubai Food Festival is the favourite event of the city's residents, who wait to experience the best in the food industry every year. From enjoying deconstructed black forest cakes, to ice creams made from frozen nitrogen, The Dubai Food Festival is a celebration of world cuisine and a true gastronomic journey bringing together world-renowned chefs, master connoisseurs and bakers.

Dubai International Kite Festival

A display of colour and art in the blue skies of Dubai, the Dubai International Kite Festival motivates kite flyers from around the world to bring their best to Dubai. Held at Jumeirah Beach behind Sunset Mall, the festival fills the open air with kites of different colours, sizes and designs. The event is free and open to the public. The festival is now a ming to bring together kite players for an annual championship for kite flyers, making the festival the first of its kind in the region.

Middle East Rail 2016

This is the longest-running and most successful railway event in the Middle East, bringing to the region the latest in the global rail industry – latest technologies, challenges and information from the industry. The event is attended by over 600 delegates from organisations like Dubai Metro, Etihad Rail, Qatar Rail, Oman Rail, Saudi Railways Organization (SRO), Saudi Railway Company (SAR), Egyptian National Railways and many more.

Dubai International Horse Fair

Dubai International Horse Fair is the only trade and consumer show where suppliers can meet owners, breeders, stables, clubs, and veterinarians, and attend one of the most important Arabian horse competitions on the global calendar. The exhibition features local and international suppliers of horse riding gear, endurance equipment, accessories and the best solutions in equine care.

Dubai International Property Show

Since its inception in 2001, the Dubai International Property Show has been the region's foremost property marketplace to meet and to do business with key real estate developers, regional and international investment promotion authorities, architects, designers and other real estate professionals. Held in conjunction with the Annual Investment Meeting (AIM), under the patronage of His Highness Sheikh Mohammed bin Rashid Al Maktoum, Vice-President and Prime Minister of UAE and the Ruler of Dubai, the International Property Show offers the perfect platform to explore the best local and international investment opportunities in the real estate market.

GITEX Technology Week

GITEX can be easily considered the most awaited technology exhibition and sale of Dubai. With over two decades of success behind it, GITEX has manufacturers displaying their latest products and technologies directly to their end users. Due to the high demand, GITEX Shopper is held annually and is the largest consumer IT and electronics sales exposition in the Middle East.

Standard Chartered Dubai Marathon

The most covered marathon, The Standard Chartered Dubai Marathon and Dubai Half Marathon has been organised in Dubai since 2000 under the patronage of His Highness Sheikh Mohammed bin Rashid Al Maktoum, bringing together sports and athletic enthusiasts from Dubai and across the world.

Ramadan Night Market

Held during the Holy Month of Ramadan, the Ramadan Night Market offers great bargains and night shopping after Iftar to the residents who start shopping prior to Eid. The market is a showcase of clothing, jewellery and accessories, health and beauty products, personal care items, perfumes, food, home appliances, electronics, toys and baby items, handicrafts, souvenirs and collectibles, travel and tourism offers, medical items and much more. The feel of a *souq* open

Tourist souvenirs on display, spanning a huge range of items.

late after midnight makes it attractive for shoppers during Ramadan.

Emirates Classic Car Festival

The classic car show returns to Dubai hosting some of the most memorable and finest old automobiles in the region. The Emirates Classic Car Festival brings some of the finest, rarest and most exquisite classic cars and their proud owners together for an exhibition that is in its eighth year. Take a look at some of the most beautiful cars and motorbikes and witness the evolution of automobiles. The Emirates Classic Car Festival is regarded as the Middle East's premier showcase of classic cars. The festival is organised by Emaar Properties in association with the Automobile & Touring Club of the UAE (ATCUAE), with the support of the Ministry of Culture, Youth & Community Development and the Roads & Transport Authority. The festival also drew the support of the Fédération Internationale des Véhicules Anciens (FIVA), and various museums and classic car owners after it moved to downtown Dubai. If you would like to exhibit your Pre-1986 classic car, truck or a motorbike, you can participate in Emirates Classic Car Festival 2016.

The Emirates Classic Car Festival was initially staged at Dubai Festival City and is now annually held on Mohammed bin Rashid Boulevard, a spectacular boulevard that looks onto Burj Khalifa, the world's tallest building, in downtown Dubai. Classic car enthusiasts from across the UAE and the wider region take part in the event. The festival brings together an amazing collection of classic cars that also opens doors to the history of evolution of the global automobile industry.

Dubai World Cup 2016

Horseracing began in the Emirate in October 1981, when the dusty Camel Track hosted the first thoroughbred race meeting. Three races were run – a sprint, a mile and a mile and a half, organised by the office of His Highness Sheikh Mohammed bin Rashid Al Maktoum. The region's premier equestrian event pays tribute to the Arabian love affair with horses and is also one of the UAE's biggest social and sporting events. Taking place on the last Saturday of March at the iconic Medan Racecourse, it is the richest day of racing in the world with a combined prize purse of US$ 30 million. Last year's event featured nine races, highlighted by the US$ 10 million Dubai World Cup sponsored by Emirates Airline.

Beach Polo Club

Beach Polo adds an electrifying dimension by swapping turf for surf as players battle it out on the sands of one of Dubai's iconic beach locations. The Beach Polo Cup Dubai 2016 will celebrate its ongoing success by bringing an entourage of professional polo players from around the world, as well as celebrities from the region. Having been featured in 32 cities around the world, this is the 12th edition of the competition.

A parade along JBR (Jumeirah Beach Residence) marks the official start of the tournament and will be attended by the four participating teams. composed of Emirati and international players.

Dubai Tango Festival

The Dubai Tango Festival returns for its eighth edition. It's the night to connect tango lovers from all over the globe here in Dubai. The four-day festival will feature various tango

workshops, milongas, an unparalleled tango night and gala dinner. Live music will be played every night by some of the most talented tango musicians and singers, and also showcase some gorgeous performances.

Under the patronage of H.E. Ruben Caro, Ambassador of Argentina, the Dubai Tango Festival Team welcomes you to the Tango Gala Dinner.

Dubai Sports World

If you're passionate about sports, then this is where you belong. For two and a half months, Dubai Sports World packs the globe's favourite sports into the emirate's largest indoor summer sports venue, offering sports enthusiasts in Dubai a chance to enjoy their favourite sports indoors during the summer heat. One of the biggest indoor playing fields, the venue includes football, basketball, volleyball, tennis courts and more. Book a court with mates or simply join in with other players and enjoy your favourite sports in the middle of summer in an indoor setting. Spanning more than 20,000 m² (215, 278.2 sq ft) of air conditioned space; Dubai Sports World will host numerous academies and sports enthusiasts of all ages, covering a range of activities, fitness programmes and events - all summer long.

Whether you're a recreational athlete, a professional or a spectator, you can connect with your sport in the way you like best. Rent a court or pitch and get your friends and colleagues together for a friendly match. Join a leading sports academy and brush up on your sporting skills. Or bring your club and challenge your competitors in the ultimate showdown. Whether you like to get fit, play for fun or play to win, Dubai Sports World caters to every level of skill and devotion. Dubai Sports World is organised by Dubai World Trade Centre in association with Dubai Sports Council.

Modhesh World
Touted as the largest indoor family theme park during the summer in Dubai, Modhesh World has grown over the years to become a destination by itself, attracting around 500,000 visitors in previous editions. The annual family event aims to bring innovative and exciting entertainment to the whole family, and includes attractions such as action-packed rides, international acts, games and activities.

Dubai Summer Surprises
After the success of Dubai Shopping Festival, Dubai Summer Surprises (DSS) kicked off in the summer of 1998 to market Dubai as a tourist destination not just in the winters but also in summer months. The Dubai Summer Surprises calendar is fully geared to keeping families with children entertained during their summer holidays in Dubai. Every mall has a variety of events and attractions lined up

for the Dubai Summer Surprises that change every week. Malls offer great sales during this time coupled with many lucky draws and competitions for both parents and children of all age groups.

Dubai Music Week

Starting from 2013, Dubai Music Week is a premium musical festival of the Middle East attracting an award-winning lineup of A-list performers, celebrity guest speakers, master classes and an interactive entertainment village. The festival draws the best performers in the industry, celebrating a variety of musical forms like rock, pop, urban, Arab, Latin and classical jazz, and bringing music heavyweights to fans.

Local musical groups are also given a platform to showcase their talent. Limited master classes led by globally recognised experts in vocals, dance, drums and guitar attract music lovers to The Music Week, an interactive festival of music which hosts music and cutting edge gaming experiences with a great variety of food and beverage options at the venue. Visitors also get a chance to experience brands and services from the entertainment, music instruments, musical education, e-commerce, audio equipment, art and lifestyle industries.

Dubai International Dance Festival

The Dubai International Dance Festival is a unique multi-arts event and has a reputation for attracting well-known dance companies, classical dance academies, youth orchestras, bands, and music ensembles from around the region and the world.

The Festival is also a catalyst for the creation of new work and creative activity, with an education programme and artistic collaborations with organisations throughout the UAE, the Middle East, and the rest of the world.

Gulf Bike Week

Gulf Bike Week is the region's premiere event featuring not only bikes and the biking lifestyle, but music and much more. Experience daring bike stunts, drifting sequences and some of the coolest and most unique motorbikes at Gulf Bike Week.

Dubai Design Week

The new kid on the block, the Dubai Design Week held in partnership with Dubai Design District (d3) is held under the Patronage of Her Highness Sheikha Latifa bint Mohammed bin Rashid Al Maktoum, Vice-Chairman of Dubai Culture & Arts Authority. Dubai Design week is an attempt to provide a platform to the designers of the region, aiming to place Dubai as a capital for fashion and art designers. The Dubai Design Week is planned with several activities and projects for registered designers.

World Tour Championship

The DP World Tour Championship is a world-class sporting and social event and the final tournament of the European Tour's Race to Dubai – a season-long competition spanning 45 tournaments in 26 destinations and across all five continents on the 2016 European Tour International Schedule. Now celebrating its eighth year, the championship hosts the top 60 golfers on the European Tour on the Earth course at Jumeirah Golf Estates, Dubai.

DUBAI'S HIDDEN SECRETS
Bait Al Wakeel

Considered to be Dubai's first office building to the restaurant extraordinaire it is today, Bait Al Wakeel is an important part of Dubai's history. Bait Al Wakeel was commissioned by the late Sheikh Rashid bin Saeed Al Maktoum (father of the current Ruler of Dubai, His Highness Sheikh Mohammed bin Rashid Al Maktoum) in 1934. The restaurant is located in downtown Bur Dubai, nestled between narrow alleyways. It features a quaint, rustic dining environment to savour classic Arabic fares, including *shish tawook*, *shawarmas*, *manakish* and seafood. Spending a relaxed evening at the Bait Al Wakeel is a delight for anyone who wants to relish the times gone by, the rustic charm of the *abras* and watching the peaceful waters of the creek. Call Bait Al Wakeel at (971) 4353-0530 to confirm timings and table availability.

Art Room Hotel in Bastakiya

Dubai has a mysterious and classical level of art that inspires its creative minds. The XVA Art Hotel is a gem hidden right inside the alleyways of Bastakiya. This hotel is not for the regular sightseeing tourist but for the artist who would like to soak in the traditional piece of art. The XVA Art Hotel consists of just six rooms and was once an old Arabic home that has been renovated to offer the feel of a traditional home with a *majlis*, open courtyards, wind towers and Arabic decor. Tip: if the artist in you isn't tired enough to crash by 9:00 pm, take a walk around the neighborhood to explore the traditional way of Emirati living, very far from the skyscrapers. Local Arabs gather around after dinner to talk and relax over tea at the *majlis* and are very hospitable to invite visitors to join them. Contact

XVA Gallery for viewing and room booking at (971) 4353-5383 or (971) 56884-7735.

Dubai Astronomy Group

The young city of Dubai has its own Dubai Astronomy Group that is a group of enthusiastic amateur astrologers who organise regular meet ups and star gazing events. Great fun for both kids and adults, watching stars and constellations from the clear desert skies are a delight for astronomers. The Dubai Astronomy group gathers regularly at their observatory, The Zubair Astronomy Camp. Details can be found on their website www.dubaiastronomy.com. Contact Dubai Astronomy Group at (971) 50624-6172.

Boating in Zabeel Park

Not a secret but yet such a relief from the summer heat to see a boating pond right inside the middle of the park located in the heart of the city. For all those funholics who want to steer their own boat for a ride, the boating pond leases electric boats that have a simple joystick for steering around the pond for thirty minutes, enough to circle around the pond 10 to 15 times. Call Zabeel Park at (971) 4324-3332.

Ras Al Khor Wildlife Sanctuary

Dubai's open secret is located in the middle of the city. Ras Al Khor Wildlife Sanctuary is the only urban protected area in Dubai. The Ras Al Khor Wildlife Sanctuary is home to over 1,500 flamingos that make for a specular view set against the backdrop of the Dubai skyline. To keep too many visitors from disturbing the wildlife, the sanctuary has a small viewing entrance which makes it even more serene and calm. The Ras Al Khor Wildlife Sanctuary is located opposite the Emarat garage on the E66 Highway (aka Oud Metha Road). Call 04-2064240 to arrange permits.

Chalets at Mamzar Beach

A simple yet comfortable chalet by beach at only AED 200 (US$ 55). Crazy as it may sound; the chalets at the Mamzar beach are available to be leased. However the drawback is the bookings are made more than a year in advance which makes it hard to get last minute confirmation.

Chill Out Lounge Dubai

When the summer heat gets on and the temperatures move up, this place is a must-go. Bringing the impossible into Dubai, the Chill Out Lounge offers a freezing experience to its inquisitive visitors. At the entrance, visitors are offered warm thermal jackets and gloves to keep them warm once they walk into the lounge. The lounge does not serve big meals but offers a great selection of hot chocolate, coffees and teas. The temperatures are sub-zero and the interiors are furnished with ice seatings, sculptures and furniture. Chill Out Dubai also organises group events, birthday parties and corporate events. Call (971) 4341-8121 or visit www.chilloutdubai.com

Desert Drummers

This is one of the favourite must-do experiences for visitors to Dubai. Created by Julian-Ann Odell, a life coach who revolutionised the concept of drumming in Dubai, the Desert Drummers organise full moon drumming with hundreds of people drumming to the same tune in the desert. Drumming together in a group is a super stress buster, corporate team building exercise, community gathering and lots of fun and laughter. Desert Drummers also offer drum classes and team events for corporates, schools and larger groups. Visit Desert Drummers on www.dubaidrums.com or call 050-6592874.

Sheikh Saeed House

Built in 1896 and located by the Dubai Creek in the Shindagha area of Bur Dubai, Sheikh Saeed house was the residence of the Al Maktoum family. The classic home of the late Sheikh Saeed (grandfather of the current Ruler, His Highness Sheikh Mohammed bin Rashid Al Maktoum) is a classic example of domestic Arabian architecture, complete with picturesque wind towers. Today, the Sheikh Saeed house is used as a heritage museum where historic photography, currency, coins, jewellery and other household items are displayed.

The sweeping views of the Dubai skyline found on the top floor give the entire experience a travelling-through-time feeling. One of the properties located close to the Sheikh Saeed house is the Horse Museum that has a large courtyard overlooking the rooms and divans. Call (971) 4393-7139 to get details or book a tour session.

The Scene Club

There's a world of cinema beyond Hollywood at The Scene Club. Watch an uncensored independent film in its raw form from a new country each month with topics that are debatable and impactful, followed by an open Q&A with a member of the cast or crew. The Scene Club was founded in 2007 by an Emirati award-winning director, Nayla Al Khaja. It is a non-profit film club that aims to showcase the best of international independent cinema. Get in touch with The Scene Club at Knowledge Village Conference Centre, Dubai, at 04-3439101.

Quad Biking

Drive outside Dubai towards Hatta and you will surely find quad bikes for hire to ride over sand dunes. Leasing rate differ

depending on the size, season and weekday. Smaller bikes can be hired for AED 300 (US$ 100) and weekend rates can be around AED 500 (US$ 150). The minimum age to hire the quad bikes is 15 years. Young adventurers are required to be accompanied by an adult. If required, training sessions are available. Most tourists are thrilled to experience exploring the sand dunes on the quad bikes as it raises adrenaline levels. Contact one of the many quad biking rentals at (971) 55912-3045 or email: info@quadbikeindubai.com.

Camel Racing Events

If you happen to be in Dubai during winter, camel racing events happen on weekends in the morning and early evening. Enjoy the camels as they gracefully race through their set tracks. Child jockeys who were previously used are now banned and replaced by robotic jockeys. Call (971) 4832-6526 to find out details of the next race.

Al Reef Bakery

For anyone who has ever ventured out late at night, Al Reef Bakery is the hidden gem that Dubaians are very proud of because it caters to their hunger 24/7, 365 days a year. Al Reef Bakery serves freshly baked cheese and zatar breads. Al Reef Bakery has one branch at Karama and another one at Al Wasl Road, among other locations. Don't be surprised to find Al Reef Bakery busy even at midnight, serving its best bread. Call (971) 4394-5200.

Camel Market

Dubai's Camel market is called Lisaili, located next to the Dubai Racing Club on the Dubai Al-Ain road. The market is a collection of tiny retail shops that sell camel blankets, canes and ornaments to dress up the camels. The adult camels can be seen wearing brightly colored, woven nose cones. The market particularly specialises in products such as camel fodder, medications and accessories like ropes, blankets, canes and camel jockey outfits. The market serves camel riders looking to buy and sell these racing animals. The camel market is a wonderful testament to the ancient Arabic culture and is a must-visit to understand the camel heritage of the UAE. It is best to visit it in the early morning to get a glimpse of how the shopkeepers set up the market and see the camels being adorned with accessories or lined up for a mock race.

TOURIST MUST-DO'S

Dubai has become a Mecca for tourism, having built an infrastructure that matches anywhere else in the world, although don't be fooled into thinking Dubai is just like the West, with an exotic twist. Dubai is not just a city where the rich head for an indulgant break or a once-in-a-lifetime holiday. There are also several budget tours available for travellers at the lower end of the spectrum.

iFLY at Mirdif Mall

Located in Mirdif City Centre, iFLY allows visitors to experience the thrill of skydiving without having to jump from a plane at 20,000 ft (6,096 m). With experienced flight instructors and its state-of-the-art simulator, one will be able to truly experience the freefall of skydiving, in a safe environment.

Chill Out Lounge at Times Square Shopping Mall

Chill out at this sub-zero temperature lounge where the tables, chairs, and even the plates and glasses are made from ice. With everything provided to keep you warm and cozy, it's a great place to chill out after an afternoon in the desert.

Khan Murjan

Experience local Arabic street shopping at Khan Murjan, situated at the underground of Wafi City Centre mall, reminiscent of a 14th century Baghdad *souq*. Khan Murjan houses 150 stores that sell souvenirs that tourists can take back home, local ware, crafts and jewellery.

Autodrome

For every car enthusiast, racing at the Dubai Autodrome is a must on the to-do list in Dubai. The Dubai Autodrome also caters to corporate events, birthday parties and offers group discounts. The Dubai autodrome has both an indoor and outdoor karting zone and accepts guests over the age of eight years. Experience the thrills and excitement of getting behind the wheel of a professional race car.

Karama Shopping District

Many in Dubai can vouch that Karama is the destination to pick the best bargains in Dubai. From shops that offer a whole range of household wares for AED 3 (US$ 0.82) to ladies' salons to furniture and mobile phones, the Karama market has it all inside its little area.

Moroccan ceramics, a favourite tourist souvenir.

Global Village

Opened alongside the Dubai Shopping Festival, Global Village opens its doors to visitors from November to February making it the largest seasonal shopping, gaming and cultural destination that brings together participants from seventy countries from around the world. Take a hired car or a local resident along as it is located some way from the residential areas.

Sega Republic

The first indoor theme park of the region, Sega Republic at Dubai Mall offers five zones of entertainment spread over two levels offering nine major rides and 250 games with adrenaline pumping attractions and games providing family fun for all ages. Passes are available for unlimited rides and games.

KidZania

A children's entertainment theme part that was first established in Mexico in 1999 has made its way to Dubai at the Dubai Mall. A big relief for parents, KidZania is the perfect theme park to drop the kids where they try out different professions experiencing what it is like to be a grown up in that profession and earn money to spend within the park. From simulating what it would be like to be a pilot, to the experience of being a top model, there are 75 professions from which to choose.

Bab Al Shams

Bab Al Shams which means 'Gateway to the Sun' is a five star desert resort located on the outskirts of Dubai, designed to give guests the authentic feel of a local Arabic home.

Included in the resort are a spa and other cultural experiences like open-air dining, falconing and camel rides among other ways to enjoy true Arabic hospitality.

Wild Wadi

Wild Wadi, themed on a mythical Arab explorer called Juha and his chum Sinbad, is Dubai's water park located next to the Jumeirah Beach Hotel. It is a veritable celebration of cellulite, and you'll find all nationalities enjoying themselves, dressed in a range of attire from the skimpiest G-string bikini to fully clothed (including a veil), and everything in between. It's a superb day out for those more than 1.1 metres (3.6 ft) tall, whether they're five or 85. Operating on a cashless system where credit is loaded onto a wrist-watch type strap, which also acts as a key to your locker, more than 20 rides propel visitors round the park's 12 acres (48,562.3 sqm).

The Jumeirah Sceirah at Wild Wadi is believed to be the fastest and tallest free fall slide outside the US; other rides include Master Blaster slides, uphill water roller coasters that pummel your bottom, the Lazy River, and the Flood River, with its surprise waves.

ENJOYING DUBAI WITH AED 10

Take a walk around the serenity of the many parks in Dubai. Parks include Zabeel Park, Mamzar Park and Safa Park, are open from 7:00 am to 9:00 pm and have an entrance fee of AED 5 only.

1. Enjoy the yachts and breeze around Dubai Marina.
2. Watch the Dubai Fountain that reaches 500 ft (152.4 m) in height and can spray up to 83,000 litres (21,926.3 gallons) of water into the air. And it costs nothing!

3. Visit the Art Galleries at DIFC. With six art galleries displaying works from both local and international artists, you can spend half a day just admiring the art at the galleries at DIFC.

4. Watch the flamingos from the Ras Al Khor wildlife sanctuary in Dubai. This protected area in Oud Metha street of Dubai is a natural home to over 1,500 flamingos. No fees to watch the flamingos.

5. Take a jog or unwind with a book at Jumeirah open beach. Facilities are available for sunbathing and showers free of charge at the beach.

6. Eat a few *shawarmas* – the staple food of most Dubaians, the *shawarma* is a local sandwich priced around AED 3-5.

7. Tour a mosque for AED 10 – learn the local religion and culture.

8. Watch a movie for free under the stars every Sunday on the beanbags.

9. Cool down with ice cream – McDonald's in Dubai sells ice cream for AED 1.

THE NUTS AND BOLTS

Currency

The monetary unit of the UAE is the dirham (AED), which is divided into 100 fils. The dirham is pegged to the US dollar at the rate of AED 3.67 to US$ 1.

Electricity

Electricity in Dubai is 220 or 240 volts AC, 50Hz.

Post and Courier

Postal mail is not home delivered in Dubai. Most residents lease a box at their nearest post office where they collect their mail on a weekly basis depending on the mail expected. Dependence on postal mail is gradually reducing with the increase in most bills being received by email. Couriers companies operate efficiently for collection and delivery of packages around the city.

Domestic Help

On call domestic help is easily available in Dubai. There are several agencies that provide cleaning, baby sitting, dog walking and other domestic services. Most agencies require the staff to be hired for a minimum of four hours. The hired staff is dropped off and picked up from several locations in Dubai.

Handymen

Handymen are easy to find in Dubai. Most vendors have their own team of handymen, such as plumbers, masons, and carpenters, who can be found on the local classified websites. Bargain and decide on the rate before the job commences to save yourself being overcharged.

RRR (Recycle-Reuse-Reduce)

The recycling industry in Dubai is still in its growing stages. Steps are being taken to educate its residents and corporates on the right way of disposing waste to make it suitable for recycling. There are specific locations set up in the city to drop off different types of recyclable material like clothes, plastic, glass and e-waste.

Energy

Dubai enjoys ample sunlight throughout the year. Harnessing solar power in a city like Dubai is very feasible. Major steps are being taken to make use of solar power wherever possible. Dubai is increasingly investing in clean energy as part of its strategic plan to have solar panels on the roofs of all buildings in the city by 2030. The aim is to see solar energy account for 25 per cent of Dubai's power requirements with 7 per cent coming from nuclear power, 7 per cent from clean coal and 61 per cent from gas. By 2050, Dubai aims to have 75 per cent of its energy from clean sources making it the city with the smallest carbon footprint in the world.

LIVING LIKE A DUBAIAN

Several tourists who visit Dubai for the sun, the beach and the fine wining and dining end up setting up home in Dubai. The cosmopolitan nature of Dubai makes it a favourite destination for both working and retired adults. Dubai doesn't disappoint its residents, offering plenty of weekend entertainment, weekday activities, social and child-friendly activities year round. Visit www.vsitdubai.com for their calendar of updated information about events around the city.

Save While You Live in Dubai

Many expatriates arrive Dubai with dreams in their eyes of achieving big savings in their bank accounts, enjoying earning a tax-free income with most of their expenses taken care of by their employer. This is not really the case for many who live in Dubai, especially those with families. The dazzling lights, mouthwatering restaurant menus, classy shopping malls and endless discount offers are naturally tempting for many expatriates, making it difficult to hold on to their purse strings and maintain a disciplined savings plan while working in Dubai. Surveys conducted locally show that over 50 per cent of residents find it too hard to resist and succumb to the temptation to upgrade their lifestyle, slowly but surely: a bigger home, bigger and nicer car, more material possessions, multiple exotic holidays, the best dining options, ever expanding wardrobes filled with the priciest of designer numbers. Many expatriates end up in this endless circle of reckless spending, ending up with long credit card bills, personal loans, car loans and other liabilities over and the above the standard cost of living. Many employed professionals even with a salary of AED 25,000 (US$ 6,800) end up with zero or negative account balances at the end of the month. With no savings and not even any available emergency fund, this puts many families at risk of living on a "borrowed lifestyle". In the past, many debt-laden expatriates had to leave Dubai leaving bad loans and even their hard earned end-of-service (ESB) benefits as they become nervous over the financial mess they find themselves. A major cause of overspending has to do with the easy availability of credit cards.

Here are some tips from financial experts that can help expatriates survive in Dubai with healthy savings and balanced lifestyles:

- Buy groceries on a weekly basis in bulk from a local supermarket. Also, Spinneys offers special discounts on Mondays. A little bit of preparation goes a long way to savings over the course of a year. Invest in a big refrigerator to store food in bulk and keep them fresh.
- Pack your lunch to work instead of ordering in from a website or with your colleagues. It is healthier saves money. Spoil yourself by eating out only once or twice a week even if you are tempted to try out the fancy restaurants of Dubai.
- Participate in some of the many savings schemes available with the banks in Dubai. Forced savings are better than unintentional expenditures. You may even win it big with some of these savings schemes. Most of these bank savings schemes allow savings from AED 100 (US$ 35). Small targets are easily achievable.
- Avoid hoarding unwanted things and luxuries. Since many expatriates eventually plan to move back to their home country, avoid hoarding unwanted luxuries. Save yourself some money and also space.
- Medical insurance – although most employers in

Dubai cover employees and their families for medical expenses, some of the medicines and treatments remain uncovered. Smaller clinics charge substantially lesser compared to the big hospitals. Look around for the best clinic in case your insurance doesn't cover it. In case you are buying medical insurance, pay for what you need instead of signing up for an inflated insurance cover.

- Transport savings – with all the conveniences available in Dubai, although it is very comfortable to travel in the comfort of your car, try to use public transport like Dubai Metro and Dubai Bus. Not using a car saves on toll gate fees (*salik*), car insurance, car parking fees and a potential fine. If you have a friend or colleague living and working along the same route, try to use your cars on alternate days, thereby sharing for both.

- Car fines – be careful when you drive in Dubai to avoid unnecessary fines. As small and unnoticeable as they seem, fines can cost a lot when you accumulate several over the course of a year.

- House rent savings – living closer to your office can save you time and a lot of stress apart from petrol costs. The newer neighborhoods in Dubai have newly constructed apartments available at low rents. Furnish your apartment with economical furniture instead of splurging on over the top brands and save some dirhams in your pocket.

- Don't bother to buy a dryer while in Dubai. Dubai has ample sunshine year round to dry laundry outdoors.

- Communication expenses – landlines in Dubai come free with the Internet package. Calls between landline numbers are free in Dubai.

- Movies – most credit cards in Dubai offer discounts on movie tickets and food from the candy bar. Use the credit cards wisely and save some money.

Weekend Activities
Fishing in Dubai
Fishing was an important activity for the local people of Dubai and is a favourite pastime among the residents even today. The city of Dubai lies almost entirely along the coast and organised fishing trips are regularly arranged for individuals and groups. Some of the kinds of fish that are caught are Sheri, Hammour, grouper, barracuda, king fish and Sheri. The wide open seas, the fresh ocean breeze and freedom of being in the middle of the ocean make for a great team activity for friends and families who love to take to the seas. The best time to fish is from October to March.

Cinemas

Going to the movies is a favourite pasttime in Dubai, especially in the summer months when outdoor activities are restricted. Cinemas in Dubai show movies in multiple popular languages like English, Arabic, Hindi, Tagalog, Tamil, Malayam and Urdu.

Camel Polo

An unusual team building activity, the Dubai Polo Club offers the entertaining sport of camel polo. A group of friends riding on camels and playing polo makes it a fun day out. The Polo Club is a beautiful place with restaurants and a lovely spa to spend the day.

Shisha Flavours

Over the last few years, Dubai has seen a rise in the number of *shisha* cafes and lounges that cater to the needs of their

young clientele by offering a variety of flavours along with a range of accompaniments like teas, coffees and snacks. For some tourists coming to Dubai, it is their first experience of *shisha*. Also called *hookah* or hubbly bubbly, *shisha* is right at home in Dubai. *Shisha* cafes can be found in almost every corner of Dubai, some in the middle of the streets and others at some of the most modern, exotic cafes at hotel rooftops. In Dubai, *shisha* also offers a great social opportunity for friends to talk, relax and enjoy great conversation in a calm and relaxed ambience. Upscale *shisha* lounges go on to offer dry foot and head massages, making it an irresistible experience.

Spas

In addition to the best of the regular spa treatments on their menu, spas in Dubai offer some of the most exotic and outstanding treatments. Some of the most weird spas of Dubai include: gold sheets spa, Peruvian chocolate body treatments, Inside the Womb (the experience of being inside a mother's womb), Golf ball massages, Japanese nightingale facial (the secret ingredient in the treatment is the use of nightingale droppings apparently used by Japanese *geishas* to maintain their porcelain-clear complexions and a favourite of Victoria Beckham), yogurt wrap spa, ear candling and salt cave therapy. Set out to spoil yourself and be assured that the spas in Dubai will not let you down.

Holistic Healing

A wide range of holistic healing therapies is available in Dubai. Enjoy full moon yoga, *hathya* yoga, upside down hanging yoga, chakra healing with crystals, acupuncture, aromatherapy, colour therapy, colon hydrotherapy, quantum healing, pranic healing, ozone therapy, *reiki*, and spiritual and *theta* healing.

Kids in Dubai

For families with children, there will always be something happening in the city to keep the kids occupied, within a budget that can be managed by the family.

Posh Paws Animal Sanctuary and Petting Farm

The farm is located at the Desert Equestrian Club near the Municipality Vet Clinic in Al Khawanjee Posh Paws. Visit www.poshpawsdubai.com or call 05-02730973.

Children's City at the Creek Park

The park has ample green spaces for the kids to run, skip and fall. Camel, train and cable car rides are available. Children's City is Dubai's first educational city created with children in mind, specifically those from two to eighteen. Children can explore, discover, experiment, investigate, explore, play and learn through playing, seeing, touching and running the machines and science experiments. Children's City includes the sections Earth Sciences, Toddler's Area, Planetarium, Human Body, Nature Center, International Culture, Computer and Communication, Arts and Sciences Workshop and Al-Ajyal Theatre. Call 04-3367633.

Dubai Mall

Dubai's local mantra is "When the kids can't stay home, head to Dubai Mall." Kids never cease to be amazed by the biggest fish aquarium at the Dubai Mall as they watch different types of fish from behind the barrier. At the main entrance of Dubai Mall kids are in awe of the dinosaur created with the bones of a real life Diplodocus (estimated to be between 150 and 155 million years old). Vlisit www.thedubaimall.com or call 800 38224 6255.

Organising a Party in Dubai

There are several venues to organise parties for children in Dubai. Party organisers are available to customise themed birthday parties at different locations with different concepts to suit various budgets. From doing it yourself to hiring a pro, you will not find it hard to organise a party in Dubai. Suggested venues for children's party are Chuck E Cheese, Dubai Dolphinarium, Splash and Bounce, Mad science, Tickles and Giggles. Party supplies are available at several stores easily.

SPORTS IN DUBAI

Being a desert, there are several indoors and outdoors sports practiced in the city today. The residents in Dubai can participate and view both traditional and modern sports. From horses to camel racing to FI racing and golf, Dubai has it all when it comes to sports for the spirit of competition and leisure. Dubai is home to several sports clubs with state-of-the-art facilities that have been constructed by the UAE government and private companies so that the residents can participate in sports of their choice.

The development of Dubai Sports City has enhanced the easy availability of sports grounds and training for sportsmen in Dubai. Dubai Sports City contains the Dubai International Cricket Stadium, Spanish Soccer Schools, Els Club Golf Course, Rugby Park and Swimming Academy.

Horse Riding

Equestrian sport is an integral part of Emirati heritage and culture. Dubai is very proud to host the world's richest race offering the highest prize money, with the fireworks, glamour, fashionable women and above all, fierce competition of the best breed of horses. In 1996, the American horse Cigar won the AED 14 million (US$4 million) prize. Now in its 21st year, Dubai World Cup, held on the last Saturday of March has become an event to reckon with. Horses and jockeys compete in nine races for a collective purse of AED 110 million (US$ 30 million), including a staggering AED 36.7 million (US$ 10 million) for the lead race. RTA, the transport authority of Dubai, makes special arrangements for visitors to reach the race by taxis and buses, adding 4,000 taxis and opening up 7,800 parking slots at Medan area where the races are held. Visitors turn up at the races in stylish hats and ensembles, making it a high-end glamour event. Horse riding lessons are available for interested individuals interested in learning with the necessary equipment.

Camel Racing

Camel racing s a thrilling sport that takes place in the morning on the weekends of the winter season (October to March) – a unique sport and integral part of the local heritage. Originally called the "Ship of the Desert", camels are now found only in the outskirts of the city in the desert areas. It is a must-see race as the camel race on their lean legs on the sandy tracks with the crowds cheering with excitement. The racing takes place at special tracks around the city and the atmosphere is electric, especially during public holidays, as the camels are cheered with honking cars and local Arabic commentary in its best vocabulary over the speakers.

Football

Football (soccer), the world's most popular sport is undoubtedly the favourite sport in Dubai. Dubai has some world-class football training grounds that produce some of

the best teams. The football academy at the Dubai Sports City has a full size indoor pitch with a FIFA 2-star approved competition turf and two outdoor fields where footballers can enjoy a variety of games. The Football Academy also has a young footballer's league.

Cricket

Take a drive around the downtown side of Dubai in areas of Bur Dubai and Deira on a Friday morning in winter and you are bound to find groups of cricket enthusiasts playing the game. With the opening of the International Cricket Council at the Dubai Sports City, cricket lovers in Dubai are now able to enjoy the sport at its best. The International Cricket Council in Dubai has two full sized pitches for day and night matches including all kinds of technology tools for bowlers and batsmen. The ICC Academy is the only training complex anywhere in the world to offer South Asian, English and Australian practice turf. With a majority of the expatriate population in Dubai hailing from the Indian sub-continent, cricket is a very popular game in Dubai. Dubai has hosted the Indian Premier League (IPL) in 2014, Pakistan Super League (PSL) in 2016, and the home grown T20 league called Masters Champion League (MCL) in 2016. All formats of crickets like test cricket, one day international games, T20 international games are played in Dubai.

Golf

Tourist are drawn to Dubai's golf courses, with many finding it hard to believe green grass can survive in the desert. Dubai has over ten golf clubs and some of the best golf courses in the region. Some of the biggest names in the golf world have had tee times in Dubai. Tee times can be booked online at any of the golf clubs around the city. Three of Dubai's golf clubs are PGA championship golf courses. Most of the golf clubs offer annual membership but have a waiting list for new members. Dubai hosts the annual Dubai Desert Classic, which is a European Tour event held in March and features some of the world's best golfers competing for over AED 3.6 million (US$1 million).

Tennis

Tennis is another popular sport enjoyed by the residents in Dubai. Due to the high demand, Dubai hosts some of the best training academies. Most tennis courts can be found in private clubs and hotels with regular classes available for all levels of tennis players. Dubai hosts the annual Dubai Tennis Championships, which is an ATP and WTA event, which attracts top players who compete at the Dubai Aviation Club in February. The Dubai Duty Free Tennis Championship has been held since 1993 and attracts the world's best tennis players to Dubai. Now in its 24th year, the tournament owners and organisers Dubai Duty Free are proud of one of the most popular and competitive events on the world circuit. Spectators who come to watch the games enjoy some of the best tennis in the comfortable surroundings of the well-known Irish Village and Century Village that offer a vast variety of wining and dining options.

Rugby

The expatriate community has brought with them the love of their games to Dubai. Rugby Union that is traditionally played with teams of fifteen players has been a popular sporting event on the Dubai Calendar along with doubling up to be a corporate hospitality event. In April, the Irish Village (Dubai) holds the Six Nations Rugby Tournament, while in November and December, the world-class Dubai Rugby Sevens is held. Dubai also has home grown rugby talent in teams and clubs that offer rugby training. The Rugby Zone at the Dubai Sports city provides state-of-the-art, purpose-built facilities for rugby players, coaches and referees at all skill and development levels, including elite clubs and international teams. The Ruby academy offers players on two full-size, International Rugby Board (IRB)-standard, floodlit grass pitches, as well as one IRB-standard, outdoor artificial turf pitch and one IRB-standard, air-conditioned, indoor artificial turf pitch.

Adventure Sports

1. Bungee jumping – not many are aware that the Bungee Jump World Record was set at 151 jumps in 24 hours in Dubai. Bungee jumping that was practised as an ancient ritual "Gkol" performed in the Pentecost Island in the Pacific Archipelago of Vanuatu, has evolved and made its way into Dubai in style. Modern bungee jumping began on 1st of April (Fools' Day) 1979 in England. Bungee-mania has taken off in Dubai. If you are ready to take the leap of faith, call Dubai Autodrome to book your bungee jumping slot on 056 364 7997

2. Shark Diving – Dubai mall that is home to the world's largest aquarium and underwater zoo, offers the dare devils a chance to swim with sharks. Anyone over the age of 10 can get a short diving course and go scuba diving with the scary creatures (there are other 33,000 sea creatures in the aquarium).

3. Fly boarding and hover boarding sports which are the newest sports for the adventure seekers are available in Dubai too. The fly board is connected to a powerful jetski, the flyboard rider stands on a board connected by a long hose to a watercraft and as the jetski speeds, the flying on water fun starts. Book your fly boarding session on www.searide-dubai.com or call 055 157 8393.

4. Dubai doesn't have cliffs but it has lots of skyscrapers. In October 2016, Dubai witnessed its first Cliff Diving World Series.

5. Micro lighting – cruise the skies of Dubai with microlights where you can enjoy the best bird's eye view of the city and the coastal areas. Sessions are

available for 10 to 20 minutes. Book your session on (971) 5521-20155.

6. Dragon Boat Racing – with kilometres of beach front available, it is no surprise Dubai has its own Dragon boat club. Dragon boat practice sessions are available for early morning sessions.

7. Parasailing, also known as parascending or parakiting is available at JBR in Dubai for water enthusiasts who wish to glide through the air wearing an open parachute while being towed by a motor boat. Call (971) 4399-9005 to book your paragliding experience.

8. Zip lining across Dubai – The X line is the last adventure sport to enter the Dubai adventure sports scene. The current crown prince, Sheikh Hamdan bin Mohammed bin Rashid Al Maktoum, was the first person to zip line through the Emaar boulevard. Zip-lining has taken off as the next big adventure experience in Dubai. Call (971) 4346-0003.

9. Sky Diving in Dubai – Skydive Dubai offers tandem jumps, which allow divers to experience the thrill of free falling with no previous experience while being harnessed to an instructor. The tandem jump is a great introduction to skydiving from Palm Dubai drop zone. Call (971) 4377-8888 to book your sky diving experience in Dubai.

10. IFly Dubai is for anyone who wants to experience the thrill of flying like a bird in a creative setting of indoor skydiving. IFly is a simpler version of skydiving and divers are supported by an upward windstream that can reach 220 kmph, lifting the divers up in a vertical acrylic glass wind tunnel that is 10 metres high.

Instructors are available to guide during the flight. Book your iFly experience at (971) 4231-6292.

Other Sports

Among the other popular sports found in Dubai are shooting, archery, polo, bowling and water based sports.

CINEMA

Dubai shows many of the latest blockbusters – it even showed censored versions of the controversial *The Passion of the Christ* and *The Da Vinci Code* – but unfortunately, many cinemagoers' experiences are disrupted by those who refuse to turn off their mobile phones during the film. In addition, disruptive patrons will also flood the screen with scribbles of red light from their laser pens, especially during "intimate" scenes, such as when actors of different genders hold hands.

EATING OUT

There is an eclectic choice of dining options available, but for residents, Friday brunch is a revered and much-loved Dubai institution. For a fixed price, ranging from AED 65 (US$ 17.70) to AED 395 (US$ 107.50), you can seriously overindulge on real pig bacon and eggs, along with several complimentary alcoholic drinks, followed by a traditional Sunday roast, with all the trimmings; or slurp down top-brand champagne while nibbling on delicate canapés, followed by a traditional English breakfast and a Sunday roast if you've got the stomach room. An all-day affair beginning from around 11.00 am, there's often entertainment for the kids and special children's food areas, replete with small serving dishes, colorful tables and chairs and, quite often, TVs showing cartoons.

WHAT'S NEW
Value Added Tax
Dubai, along with the rest of GCC (Gulf Cooperation Council) is gearing up to introduce VAT in 2018. VAT will initially be introduced on luxury goods and services. Foods items, healthcare and education will be exempt from VAT. There will no income taxes and no wealth taxes or property taxes.

Legoland
Under the supervision of Dubai Parks and Resorts, LEGOLAND® Dubai and LEGOLAND® Water Park opened in Dubai in October 2016. The two parks aim to become the ultimate destination in the Middle East for families with children, boasting hands-on experiences and LEGO® themed adventures through interactive rides, water slides, models and building experiences. As the first LEGOLAND® theme park in the Middle East and the seventh worldwide, LEGOLAND® Dubai will bring the well-known LEGO® brick to life in a unique interactive world specifically designed for children aged 2-12, encouraging them to stretch their imaginations and their skills as the "heroes" in a fun day spent together with friends and family. LEGOLAND® Dubai will feature over 15,000 LEGO models made from more than 60 million LEGO bricks and over 40 interactive rides, shows and attractions – all set in six themed areas.

Bollywood Park
With a Taj Mahal replica and 800-seat theatre, the Bollywood Park opened in October 2016. Bollywood will come to life for the first time in the Middle East at Bollywood Parks™ Dubai. With performances and entertainment themed in Bollywood

style, visitors will be able to experience the vibrant celebration of Mumbai's famous film industry and celebrate quintessential film flair at the retail outlets, Bollywood themed restaurants and flamboyant cinematic rides.

Motiongate Dubai

The flagship theme park is a proud venture of Dubai Parks and Resorts that has united for the first time, three holiday giants: Sony Pictures Studios, DreamWorks Animation and Lionsgate, bringing the ultimate cinema theme park to Dubai. Motiongate covers an area of 176,515.8 sqm (1.9 million sqft) filled with rides, shows, restaurants and Hollywood themed movies. The park will be spread in five different zones – Sony Pictures Studios, DreamWorks, Lions gate, Smurfs Village and Studio Central. A multipurpose theatre with a 1,000 seating capacity is also part of the park.

13 Hollywood movie franchises will make the park an adventure and action-packed experience for its visitors.

Franchises include *Cloudy with a Chance of Meatballs*, *Ghostbuster's*, *The Smurfs*, *Underworld* and *Zombie land*, *How to Train your Dragon*, *Kung Fu Panda*, *Madagascar*, *Shrek, Step-up, The Hunger Games, The Green Hornet* and *Hotel Transylvania*.

Dubai Video Game Theme Park

Dubai video game theme park is an indoor theme park located at Dubai's City Walk. Based on the makers of iconic video games such as Street Fighter, Metal Gear Solid and Final Fantasy. Meraas, the development company behind Dubai Video Games theme park is working with video game developers including Capcom, Konami, Square Enix and Electronic Arts. The Dubai video game theme park is expected to be spread over an area of about 15,000 sqm (161,458.7 sqft). A first of its kind in the region, the video game theme park at Hub Zero is yet another ambitious project in Dubai.

Riverland

Riverland is a journey through time, where four different zones have been planned to give visitors a glimpse into some of the greatest eras of the past.

The French village is a replica of a medieval French town planned and designed to look like historic architecture of Europe in the late 1600s. With towers and water wheels and authentic Mediterranean casual dining, the French village will charm and delight.

The Boardwalk is inspired by America in the 1950s with lofty structures, palm trees and glamorous neon signage, bustling with street performers, jugglers and artists all around. The American style of grab and go quick bites are available.

India Gate is planned as a royal Asian extravaganza with musicians, acrobats and mesmerising elephant sculptures that will remind you of India. With street performers and entertainment, here taste buds will get to explore Asian cuisine at its best.

The Peninsula is the heart of Riverland Dubai. Surrounded by the river, this is the place where visitors will able to enjoy various festivals and concerts at the large outdoor venue. The outdoor piazza has19th century architectural themes that connect all the different districts of Riverland via impressive bridges.

Visitors who wish to stay close to the areas of Motiongate, Bollywood Parks, LEGOLAND® Dubai, LEGOLAND® Water Park and Riverland Dubai will have the option to check in to Lapita hotel. A Polynesian themed resort, expansive pathways sprinkled with colorful flowers adorn the entrance to the Lapita™ Autograph Collection® hotel. The hotel will offer exclusive signature dining restaurants and a signature spa.

Dubai Parks and Resorts expects to sell 6.7 million tickets in its first year of operation. Spread across 2,322,576 million sqm (25 million sqft), the three world-class theme parks and water park will offer over 100 attractions in total.

CHAPTER 8

THE LANGUAGE

> *❝What is destined to reach you will reach you,
> even if it be underneath two mountains.
> What is not destined to reach you will not reach you,
> even if it's already between your two lips.❞*

— **Arabic proverb**

HISTORY OF ARABIC

Arabic is the world's fifth most spoken language and the sixth official language of the United Nations spoken by over two billion speakers. It is an ancient language widely used, from Asia to several countries in Africa. Arabic is closely related to Aramaic, Hebrew, Phoenician and Ugaritic and is the liturgical language of Muslims. The holy book of the Muslim, the Holy Quran is written in Arabic, the language used being called Quranic Arabic.

Quranic Arabic is widely taught in Arabic schools and universities and mainly at government offices. It is written from right-to-left. The modern day Arabic language is influenced by many other languages: Urdu, Hindi, Somali, Malay, Punjabi, Sindhi, Hausa, Pashto, Indonesian, Kazakh,

Bengali, Kazakh, Kurdish, Bosnian and Swahili. The European culture was also influenced by Arabic in earlier ages. The Greek language flourished in Europe, especially in science, mathematics and philosophy. As a result, due to the closeness of

Signages around the city are in both English and Arabic.

Muslim and Christian cultures, many European languages like Greek and Latin have words of Arabic origin found in them. European languages like Spanish, Catalan, Sicilian and Portuguese have traces of Arabic in them. There have been many instances of national movements to convert Arabic script into Latin script or to Romanize the language.

The spread of Islam introduced Arabic to non-Arabic countries in Persia (now Iran), Spain and North Africa. Arabic words also made their way into several West African languages as Islam spread across the Sahara. Arabic is currently used in three ways: Classical Arabic (used in the Holy Quran), Modern Standard Arabic and daily used Arabic. Daily used Arabic is not how it is written, but mainly how the language is spoken. There have been many instances of national movements to convert Arabic script into Latin script or to Romanize the language.

In the earlier ages, Arab linguists were of the opinion that to be educated and learned in Arabic was more than sufficient to be considered literate and in fact superior than being conversant in other languages. Hence in parts of the world where Arabic was spreading, students did not show any interest in learning other languages. In modern times, the educated upper classes in the Arab world have taken a nearly opposite view. Yasir Suleiman wrote in 2011 that "studying and knowing English or French in most of the Middle East and North Africa have become a badge of sophistication and modernity and ... feigning, or asserting, weakness or lack of facility in Arabic is sometimes paraded as a sign of status, class, and perversely, even education through a mélange of code-switching practices." Arab-American professor Franck Salamah went as far as to declare Arabic a dead language conveying dead ideas, blaming its stagnation for Arab intellectual stagnation and lamenting those great writers in Arabic judged by their command of the language and not the merit of the ideas they express with it.

Modern Standard Arabic is the most widely used Arabic, used by media in print today. Students and learners of the language are trained in standard Arabic which equips them to read, write and understand the language with its variants. Try observing different Arabs talking in Arabic and you may notice the difference in dialects and body language, e.g. an Egyptian talking to a Saudi or a Moroccan talking to an Emirati. The Arab youths are highly influenced by the language used in latest movies and music albums. The Arabic theatre uses the modern day language as well.

The Various Types of Arabic

1. Egyptian Arabic spoken by around 55 million people and the most widely spoken and understood, owing to the widespread interest in Egyptian movies, music and drama shows.

2. Gulf Arabic spoken mostly by GCC locals who include UAE Emiratis, Kuwaitis, Qataris, Omanis and Saudis. It is interesting to note that many Qatari speak in Najdi Arabic as well.

3. Hejazi Arabic mostly spoken in the Western parts of Saudi Arabia.

4. Maghrebi Arabic, called "Darija" is spoken by Moroccans, Algerians, Libyans and Tunisian. There is a marked difference in the dialect of Maghrebi and Gulf Arabic. The closest is the language spoken by Libyans, followed by Tunisians and Algerians. Moroccan spoken Arabic is the farthest from the Gulf Arabic Iraqi. Aamiyah or Mesopotamian Arabic is spoken in Iraq and parts of Iran and Syria.

5. People in Azerbaijan also spoke in a dialect called Shirvani Arabic until the late 1930s. However Shirvani is now an extinct language.

6. Muslims in Portugal and Spain spoke Andalusian Arabic.

ARABIC LANGUAGE ENTERTAINMENT

Arabic movies are made in Algeria, Morocco, Syria, Tunisia, UAE and Egypt. Egyptian cinema has been the most active of the Arabic cinema industry. The first Arabic movie was made in Egypt in 1925. The University of North Carolina claims to have the most comprehensive and diverse collection of films and videos of the Middle East and Islamic world with more than 500 titles on the list.

Try a bit of Arabic

Keif Ha-Laq	How are you?
Sabah Al Khair	Good morning
Masah Al Khair	Good evening
Yallah	Come on
Nam-shi:	Let's go
Aiya Keemat:	What's the price?
Ahlan Wa Sahlan	Welcome
Iftah	Open
Ismek Al Kareem	What is your name?
Fadal	Please
Kabeer	Big
Sagheer	Small
Madrasa	School
Mabrook	Congratulations
Min Fadlik	Excuse me?
Kam Alsaa	What is the time?
Tatakkellem ingleezi?	Do you speak English?
Mafi Mushkil	No problem
Wayn Hammam	Where is the loo?
Taal Bukra	Come tomorrow
Kam Ijara?	What is the rent?

A BILINGUAL CITY

Although Arabic is the national language of Dubai, English is widely spoken and understood by all. You will never find yourself in a situation with no one understanding English in this city. Road signs, retail store boards, commercial vehicles all have information in both English and Arabic.

LEARNING THE LOCAL LANGUAGE

Most of the youth of the current generation are used to Modern Standard Arabic. There are several institutes that offer Arabic classes for reading, writing and spoken Arabic. There is a lot of difference between the classical theoretical Arabic and the spoken Arabic slang. Taking Arabic language classes will certainly help you understand the dialect and communicate with people around more easily. Studying Modern Standard Arabic will help you acquire a good combination of the colloquial as well classical Arabic and yet be able to converse with various Arabic speakers. Modern Standard Arabic is used in informal speeches and interviews. Another common option is learning Egyptian Arabic, which is the most comprehensible dialect in the region.

It is hard to get the dialect if you are not a native Arab. However, many expatriates in UAE make a sincere effort to learn the language as part of settling down. One of the popular training centres is the Arabic Language Centre at the Dubai World Trade Centre, which offers courses from beginner to advanced level for general conversation. They also offer some courses for specific industries such as tourism, health or finance.

If you are looking for more personalised courses, you can also hire a private teacher. This option is preferred by many expatriates.

CHAPTER 9

WORKING IN DUBAI

> One of the main characteristics that differentiates Dubai from other commercial centres is its openness to innovation and the freedoms it grants people and institutions to operate.

— **Abdul Aziz Al Ghurair, CEO of Mashreq Bank**

WORK CULTURE
Business Etiquette

In the UAE, Islam is more than a religion; it is a way of life which is reflected throughout the culture, laws and attitudes of the people. Although Dubai is now viewed as relatively tolerant and cosmopolitan due to the large number of expatriates living here, it is essential that everyone living here is sensitive and behave appropriately when conducting business in the UAE. Whether you are relocating to the UAE permanently or you are on a business trip, it's important to be aware of these cultural differences in order to organise or

View of Dubai's corporate district, Sheikh Zayed Road.

partake in successful business meetings or develop potential partnerships.

Dressing for Work

In a place where women stalk the malls in stilettos, don't be surprised if you feel under-dressed in Dubai. Women in Dubai do make an effort to dress to impress. From designer bags to much needed sunglasses, manicured nails and the perfect no-sweat makeup, women in Dubai are glamorous, confident and yet modest in their dressing choices. Suits, shirts, trousers, knee length skirts are favourite formal wear choices. Men keep it professional with half or full sleeved shirts and smart trousers. Basically, dress modestly with class and you are in Dubai's corporate world. As a women, dress up with knees, shoulders and arms covered. This is well respected by the Arab men. You can flaunt your best pair of shoes in Dubai. Shorts and tees are best left for weekends. Wearing clothes that are too revealing is not considered a sign of respect and professionalism. Avoid informal footwear like flip flops, sandals or sneakers at work.

Working Days

When conducting business in the UAE, it is important to know that Muslims pray five times a day: at dawn, midday (after the sun passes its highest point), the late part of the afternoon, just after sunset and between sunset and midnight. This means that you will need to schedule your business meeting outside these times to avoid disruption and disrespect.

Another point to remember is that in the UAE, the working week does not begin on Monday and end on Friday, but instead the first day of the week is Sunday and their last day is Thursday. Friday is the Muslim day of prayer and rest known as Jummah.

Liquor

Being an Islamic city, don't expect to be served alcohol during any business meetings in Dubai. Although non-Muslims who hold liquor licenses are allowed to consume alcohol, it is advised to respect the local culture and not offer any form of alcohol or spirit to locals and Muslims who may take offense to the same. In terms of food habits, be mindful that Muslims do not consume pork. Personal relationships and family ties are built up on mutual friendship, trust and respect. The foreign employee may seem at a disadvantage in this regard, which is why first impressions are so important. Contacts and friends in the right places can act as stepping stones to greater success, so any relationship built in the business circle should be treated with the utmost respect. It is also worth noting that if you are granted a favour this will not be forgotten and it is expected that you reciprocate this generosity.

Doing Business During Ramadan

If your business trip coincides with the month of Ramadan, you need to know that the strict fast applies to everyone, even non-Muslims. During the daylight hours, Muslims from all over the world abstain from food and drink. There are however, many large hotels which have special screened off areas for non-Muslims to eat and drink, with the exception of alcohol.

At the beginning of Ramadan, it is courtesy to greet those observing Ramadan with the following phrases: "Ramadan Kareem!" meaning "noble Ramadan" or "Ramadan Mubarak!" meaning "blessed Ramadan".

Some Useful Expressions

It's always useful to have a couple of expressions under your belt when conducting business in the UAE because this not only shows your interest in their culture, but also demonstrates a respectful attitude. The customary greeting is "As-salam alaikum", meaning "peace be upon you". If replying to a greeting you should respond with "Wa alaikum as-salam" which means "and upon you be peace". When asking for some something, you should say "Min Fudlek", meaning "please", and "Shukran" for "thank you". Lastly, if you have come to a business decision and agree to proceed to the next step, say "Inshallah", meaning "God willing".

Dates, Coffee and the Handshake

As any professional would vouch, being on time is a respected professional quality. However, do not surprised if your counterpart turns up late or makes you wait. Do not take offense; it is a way of doing business in this part of the world. When you plan to conduct business in Dubai, your handshake will speak a lot about you. A confident yet not too firm grip is the starting point. Always start off with shaking hands with men first. Do not shake hands with an Arab woman unless she offers her hand first, or if you are a woman do not extend your hand for a handshake to an Arab man unless he initiates. Do not flirt, hit-on, touch, hug or talk in private with women. Don't be surprised if you get told off for doing so. Do not try and engage a woman in conversation unless you have been formally introduced. Do not ask the locals questions about his wife or other female members of his family as this considered part of their personal lives. Handshakes are considered basic manners in the corporate world like anywhere else in the world. If you would rather avoid handshakes altogether, place your right hand over your heart instead. A lot of time is spent on general talk before any business conversation can start. If your business contacts are visiting your office, offering them refreshments is considered polite and respectful. Never offer alcohol. Refrain from talking religion or politics.

It is interesting to understand the local way of doing business. Locals like to get a good bargain from any deal. Give in and see how it works wonders for your business.

For the first few meetings, do not expect a lot from your Emirati business associates. Keep a non-demanding agenda; rather work on building the relationship and rapport. This will go a long way in building your business. If you are invited for a meal or social event, accept the invitation with gratitude and even reciprocate if you can. With several Emiratis now well-educated and well versed with the international business world, you may not require a translator unless you are signing official documents.

Dubai enjoys a vibrant cooperate gift culture. Greeting cards and a large variety of gifts are exchanged during Ramadan and Eid. Check your company policy about gifts and favours.

LANDING THAT DREAM JOB

With a large part of the population being expatriate, organisations that are looking to hire are very careful on their choice of candidates, looking for the ability to adapt to working on an international team and different styles of working. There are several recruitment agencies operating in Dubai who are approached by companies for their services to find candidates with specific skills or from a specific background or language command for easier on boarding.

Dubai has requirements for the knowledge base and skill sets that expatriates can offer. Although expatriates can become almost permanent,they are still considered foreigners forever and dealt with in a controlled way. The labour law aims to create a fair balance between employers and employees so disputes can be handled amicably and with all fairness. The government is making heavy investments in education, literature, reading, social welfare, hoping to make its nationals independent and self-sufficient. With all of these developments, a large number of observers believe that Dubai will need the skills and talents of expatriates for many more years to sustain, expand and develop its vision of becoming a world-class city.

As several multinational companies operate in Dubai, the Internet will be your best tool to connect with these agencies and discuss the opportunities available for you in Dubai. You should ideally have a firm offer of employment before travelling to Dubai. Speculative visits are occasionally successful, but you need to be notably lucky and have high-grade qualifications and experience to stand any chance. In addition, you will almost certainly need knowledgeable local contacts and have done some research into the types of company which would most value your experience. Technical skills are always in demand, more specifically in the construction, oil and gas, aviation and banking industries. Although many prefer to arrive to Dubai with a job, it's only fair to be around in the city while you are looking for a job so you are available for any potential interviews immediately. Ideally you would have been interviewed in your home country and already been selected for a job before you travel to Dubai.

RECRUITMENT AGENCIES

With 85 per cent of the population being expatriate, a large number of this is the working population. Dubai has an appetite for all kinds of labour, both white and blue collar workers who work and live in Dubai for different lengths of time and develop their own goals. Expatriates do not get permanent residency irrespective of the length of their stay in Dubai. Dubai has fair labour laws for both the employer and employee. In case of any dispute, any employee can approach the Ministry of Labour to resolve issues. Expatriate workers in Dubai are dealt with fairly and paid according to their skills and experience that they bring to their jobs in Dubai and in many cases, better than what they are paid in their home country. Recruitment consultants play a vital role in placement of expatriate workers in industries that require their skills and expertise. Many consultants are engaged by the employers and once they understand the company's vision and goals, they work as middlemen with their counterparts in various countries to attract this talent to Dubai.

Recruitment consultants specialise in particular areas of work like recruitment of staff for an oil company, hotels, medical and nursing staff for hospitals, blue collar workers for the construction industry, and office staff for office jobs, among many other industries that require staff with technical and analytical skills. Normally recruitment companies do not charge anything to employees and secure their fees from their clients who are the employers. Many recruitment consultants offer websites where interested candidates can submit their CVs for free.

EMIRATISATION

As an efficient and forward looking government, Dubai has been focusing on placement of its local population in the workforce at all different levels of both government and private organisations. The government is keen to develop its people, provide options for their education and careers and guide the locals to become technically and financially independent, instead of being reliant on the government for their requirements. Hundreds of Emirati students study at government and private schools and universities in Dubai, with a large percentage of this being females. The government makes an honest and focused effort in supporting the Emirati students in whichever ways and industries they train in, from medical to the auto industry to astronomy to entrepreneurship. The government also provides scholarships to deserving candidates to attend universities abroad. Having made major investments in education and social welfare, Dubai aims to have its own educated and well-equipped labour population and companies are strongly encouraged to take on local nationals wherever possible. The Ministry of Labour and Social Affairs is active in helping local citizens find employment. As a result, locals are first offered jobs as trainees and interns before they reach out to the market to engage expatriates trainees. International students may find it hard to secure internships in Dubai as the university student population is active in filling up this requirement.

The number of expatriates required and the skills they bring along will be required to run the machinery of the fast growing city, although there will undoubtedly be changes in the number of expatriates employed and the type of skills required. For example, as long as the city keeps developing its infrastructure, the requirement for blue collar labourers would be high. At some point, when the city's planned infrastructure is in place, this requirement may vary resulting in a decline in the number of manual workers required. However skills that can be offered in the commercial development of the city may be required for several more years to come. Technical skills have an ongoing demand.

Dubai continues to attract a large number of foreigners who wish to settle down with full time employment and make Dubai their home. Trial visits to test the job market do work out for some while for others, having local contacts and possessing skills in demand in Dubai go a long way to securing that dream job. Expatriate workers who are looking at relocating to Dubai for work should be aware of ground realities of being a foreign worker and not arrive in Dubai with unrealistic expectations like attaining permanent residency or citizenship. It's best to interact with family or friends before deciding to relocate to Dubai. Your country's foreign office may be able to help as well.

ECONOMY

Although many believe that Dubai has a large part of its revenue coming from oil, Dubai has been focusing on diversifying the industries in the city to make it a self-reliant city.

The government's decision to diversify Dubai from a trade-based but oil-reliant economy to one that is service- and tourism-oriented has been paying off with great results.

Dubai's Successes

1. The Jebel Ali port, which has the world's largest man-made harbour, is a success story of the thriving shipping and re-export business using Dubai's strategic location around the global map. Jebel Ali Port, the largest marine terminal in the Middle East, is a premier gateway for over 90 weekly services connecting more than 140 ports worldwide with a cargo handling capacity targeted to hit 18 million TEU by 2018.

2. Emirates Airlines has a fleet of over 200 aircrafts and an impressive fleet of Airbus A380s, Boeing 777s and many other aircrafts. Emirates Airlines runs services to over 140 destinations worldwide in over 75 countries, handling over 50 million passengers in 2015.

3. Dubai aims to be the IT hub of the region, servicing industries such as finance and IT. The creation of Dubai Internet City, Dubai Media City forms the TECOM (Dubai Technology, Electronic Commerce and Media Free Zone Authority), which focus on the development of IT and media in the region. Some of the world's biggest names like SAP, Microsoft, Hewlett-Packard, Dell, Oracle Corporation and IBM and media organisations such as BBC, MBC, CNN, Reuters and Sky News operate in Dubai.

4. Tourism – with just a handful of luxury hotels in the nineties, Dubai today boasts the best hotels in the world. By 2017, Dubai is all set to become the world's third most popular tourist destination. Efforts from Dubai Tourism and Commerce Marketing have paid off in making Dubai a bucket list destination for tourists looking for luxury shopping, ultramodern architecture and a lively nightlife scene, with many other tourist activities for the whole family.

Temporary Jobs

In a robust and dynamic economy like Dubai, there are always plenty of contract and freelance jobs. However, interested candidates need to be aware of local regulations that govern the employment rules for temporary positons. Several industries have an ongoing requirement for staff depending on the season and their projects. Temporary job assignments are more difficult to find than full time jobs as the employees with friends and relatives try to get them in first for the available opportunities. Over the last few years several international students have found temporary jobs in Dubai to fill in a gap year. Temporary jobs can be found in various industries like the retail industry, during its periods of shopping festivals and high tourist season; hotel industry during high season and New Year's week; at ports during ship building and ship repair projects; medical industry with the opening of new hospitals; or driver positions for companies offering desert tours.

Working Women in Dubai

Traditionally, Arab women did not work outside their homes. Women have been the home owners taking care of the domestic side of life and bringing up the family. With the advent of education and the growth in awareness levels, the exposure to the world outside, this concept of the man being the breadwinner is changing more rapidly than ever. With several expatriate women working safely and comfortably in Dubai, it is certainly encouraging for the local women to venture out of their home, educating and equipping themselves with the skills and knowledge to enter their country's workforce. Thankfully, the laws in Dubai are very stringent when it comes to any form of harassment in the workplace, making it safe for women to travel, work and live independently in Dubai. Harassment is handled seriously, leading to severe punishment.

For a long time, local women preferred being in teaching jobs in order to get home to their children. But the concept of working women is now more varied in almost every industry.

Women in Dubai work in a large range of industries; from banking, medical, aviation and commerce to business, design, manufacturing and media, women are making great strides. A large majority of expatriate women now work in Dubai as doctors, bankers, consultants, engineers, oil industry specialists, in media, as lawyers, in the hotel industry and as entrepreneurs.

As women prove their mettle at the work front, many employers are now willing to bring women into the boardroom and make them part of the management team. Women rising to positions of power and influence tend to come from middle and upper echelon families. Indeed, for a woman to rise to a position of influence at work she needs the support of her family, especially the male members.

In 2015, several employers in Dubai agreed to extend the maternity leave for working women in private companies from the traditional 45 days to six months, thanks to the growing awareness of breastfeeding and stress for new mothers at work.

Many expatriate men who are allowed to bring in their families to Dubai may soon see the possibility of their female partner finding a job. However, the legal frameworks around this need to be checked. Not many employers prefer to hire women who have a restriction of working as they stay on their husband's sponsorship.

Salary and Working Conditions

Most expatriates working in Dubai agree that they are paid similar to or more than what they would earn back in their home countries. Employees in Dubai enjoy tax free salaries and other perks which differ between organisations and salary systems. Pay packages can include basic pay, housing and living allowance, medical insurance, air tickets and education assistance. This can differ depending on the organisation. Because Dubai employees do not incur any tax income on their salaries, net income is usually much greater, which is one of the major attractions of working in Dubai.

At the end of their service, expatriate workers are awarded an end of services gratuity to secure and help them get on. This is usually based on basic salary and the length of service, usually excluding any perks or bonuses. Many retirees are able to comfortably retire when they leave Dubai and go back to their home countries accumulating a reasonable financial cushion or to live out their retirement. Although many expatriates find it tempting to give in to the many areas of expenditure here, clever and disciplined employees strike the right balance.

The end of service payment is not like the provident fund system in other countries. The employer does not engage in investing this amount into any investment products and neither does the employee have access to the end of service pay prior to leaving the job assignment. This payment is made only once the employee leaves the company. Every time an expatriate employee leaves an employment, he or she is entitled to the end of services benefits. Indemnity scales usually amount to 21 days of basic pay per year of employment for the first five years and thereafter, 30 days salary per year of employment.

Working Hours and Overtime

For office workers, the work week in Dubai is 40 hours. In some private companies this can extend to 48 hours. Offices open by 8:00 am and close at 6:00 pm. Many companies offer working hours between these hours. There is no difference between summer and winter hours. During the holy month of Ramadan, the working hours are reduced from eight hours a day to six hours applicable to Muslim staff who fast during Ramadan. While previously Friday was the only day, the official government weekend in Dubai now is Friday and Saturday.

Employment Contracts

A crucial document for expatriates planning to relocate to Dubai is the employment contract. It is important to be aware of the terms and conditions outlined in the employment contract. The employment contract is drawn by the employer and sent across to the employee for agreement prior to processing of the visa and other formalities.

The employment contract includes details like detailed job description, salary, additional benefits, incidental expenses and other approved expenses, performance requirements and responsibilities of the employees. This document can be both in English and Arabic. If this contract is in English only, it is recommended to get it translated into Arabic as it is helpful in government interactions.

Traditionally, most expatriate contracts were for two years only, but it is now common for contracts to be open-ended. Employers have found that they can be held to a defined period if the employee proves unsatisfactory, and most contracts now have a termination notice period of between one and three months, or payment in lieu of notice. Contracts can be extended or renewed by mutual consent and frequently are, if all parties are happy with things as they are. It's quite common for expatriates to stay in Dubai until retirement. The retirement age in Dubai is 60 years. Thereafter, employees may be retained on a yearly basis by mutual consent. Dubai has sophisticated, computerised control of their labour force and specify job categories that are open to foreign labour. Once the work starts, the real work may be slightly different than what is mentioned in the employment contract. This can be verbally agreed on by both the employee and employer. There are some exceptions when it comes to nationals being employed, particularly in the service industries. In case of any confusion, the employee can always engage with the Ministry of Labour to verify any queries.

Medical Examination

As part of the relocation process, all expatriates are required to go through a government controlled medical examination prior to the issuance of a work residence visa

to rule out any infectious diseases like HIV and AIDS. The medical test can be extended for some categories based on their profession. e.g. the medical examination for blue collar workers from the Indian sub-continent and southeast Asia, who may have greater exposure to disease and less access to advanced medical resources in their home countries than Westerners. The AIDS test is mandatory and this includes the accompanying spouse as well. In case the medical examination reveals any of the listed diseases, the person is expelled from Dubai immediately. Once the tests are cleared positively, the medical clearance certificate is issued. The medical certificate is then used to apply for the relevant type of visa.

Labour Laws

There was previously a ban system wherein an employer could cancel the visa of the employee and place a six-month ban on the passport of the employee. During this period the person would not be entitled to work in Dubai. However labour laws have been changed in 2016. The six-month ban is now waived if the worker has skill levels classified by the ministry as 1, 2, and 3, meaning those who hold a university degree, post-secondary diploma or high school diploma, respectively. Employees are also given a special permit to change jobs once the Ministry of Labour confirms that the employing company has not provided work due to the firm being inactive for more than two months and, if the worker reports to the ministry during the company shutdown. Work permits may also be issued by the Ministry of Labour in case a labour complaint is referred by the Ministry to the labour court and final ruling is in favour of the worker who is terminated early or is owed outstanding wages less than two months of dues for end of service.

Ministry of Labour-approved standard employment contracts are focused to include the standard employment offers, terms, rights and obligations, informed consent, non-substitution of labour contract, filing the offer for eventual capture as a legal contract, termination clause and commitments by the employer. The contact can be terminated if the employer does not meet its contractual obligation to workers, if employer ceases to empower the worker to perform his/her employment duties without complying with due process, or if a worker absconds without complying with due termination process.

Occupational Hazards

In case of any accident suffered by an employee in the course of work, the employee is entitled to medical treatment and compensation.

Some work related diseases are poisoning by lead and its compounds, mercury and its compounds, arsenic and its compounds, antimony and its compounds, phosphorus and its compounds, petroleum, its derivatives and compounds, manganese and its compounds, sulphur and its compounds, chloroform or carbon tetrachloride.

The list also includes diseases resulting from radium or radio-active substances, chronic diseases of the skin and burns and glandes and anthrax.

Dismissal and Redundancy

Unless the employee has some serious altercation that requires immediate dismissal like a court or police intervention, the general rule is that employees are given three written notices prior to dismissal. The notices normally detail reason of the employee's failings or shortcomings. The employee should be deemed to have defaulted on the terms of contract. An employee cannot be dismissed or made redundant while on leave out of the country. The employee has the right to ask for reasons for dismissal and redundancy.

Dubai does not have any tradition of organised trade unions, and their formation is illegal; strikes, therefore, are virtually unknown. The intention of changing this is already under discussion, yet the right of forming unions will probably only apply to UAE nationals. It's possible to form an association within your company to make approaches on a collective basis to management, but this would have validity only within the individual company. Individual representation to the management is possible, but you will need to be understated, brave and have your return plane ticket handy! That being said, however, the Dubai International Financial Centre has its own legal system and laws, separate from those of the UAE. Under these laws, there is no ban on striking, however it is almost deemed as unnecessary to exist, as due to the generally high remuneration of the area it is unlikely to become an issue.

Repatriation of Expatriates

Upon completion of employment, employed expatriates are eligible to receive repatriation expenses to an agreed location. If the employer has initially paid for travelling expenses, moving expenses of household goods, the employer is required to do the same for the family to return to the country of origin.

STARTING A BUSINESS

Dubai has a dedicated focus that encourages new business setups, Small and Medium Enterprises (SMEs), large organisations as well as independent business houses to set up their offices in Dubai. Dubai has set up several dedicated free zones for different industries to keep companies

Here are the three things you must know before starting a business in Dubai:

1. Research
   Plan well and carry out feasibility studies of the demand for your product or services. Research on the appetite of the market for what you can offer, the areas where you will need to develop, the challenges that you may face in the process and cover the gaps. This initial research will go a long way in preparing the business plan.

2. Prepare your Business Plan
   Your business plan needs to include your goals, objectives, the product or service or industry you wish to cater to, along with details of the financials like investment, costs, expenses and other loans or liabilities of the organisation. When you apply for the license to operate in Dubai, the authorities may request to study your business plan and model.

3. The law requires that you have a local partner who holds the majority interest and can therefore control the business, which includes closing it if necessary. The partner can own 51 per cent of the company and the local is not required to make any financial contribution to the business.

together, enjoy potential synergies and use the advantage of knowledge sharing and growth. Dubai welcomes foreign investment greatly; there is very little red tape and no complicated processes which makes it amongst the most liberal around the world.

The Dubai government offers different types of business models to be chosen from by foreign investors, such as direct sale, commercial agency arrangements, branch or representative office, Limited Liability Company and special free zone investment.

The local Chambers of Commerce can advise about start-ups and are adept at cherry-picking potentially profitable newcomers to the region. Winning the confidence and support of a Chamber of Commerce will help your cause. Contact details are as follows:

- Dubai Chamber of Commerce and Industry
  Tel: (971) 4221-181
- Federation of UAE Chambers of Commerce and
  Industry, PO Box 8886, Dubai, UAE
  Tel: (971) 4212-977

CHARITY AND VOLUNTARY WORK

Whether you are visiting or a resident in Dubai, you will be heartened to see how the community comes together to support those with special needs. There are several informal charities and voluntary groups in Dubai.

Dubai Cares is a philanthropic initiative launched in 2007 by His Highness Sheikh Mohammed bin Rashid Al Maktoum to improve the life of children around the world giving them access to quality primary education. Dubai Cares shows the commitment of the government to guarantee universal primary education and to promote gender equality. Dubai

Cares reaches to 13 million children in 38 countries around the world. More information is available on www.dubaicares.ae.

Dubai Volunteering Center, an initiative by Community Development Authority is the first official Dubai Government body established to manage volunteering services in the UAE with a focus on bringing together volunteers who would like to get involved in the various community causes around the city. Dubai Volunteering Center creates volunteering opportunities, trains and develops volunteers and mentors the registered volunteers.

Other voluntary groups active in Dubai are Flea 4 Charity, K9 friends, Volunteer in UAE and Clowns who care.

CHAPTER 10

FAST FACTS

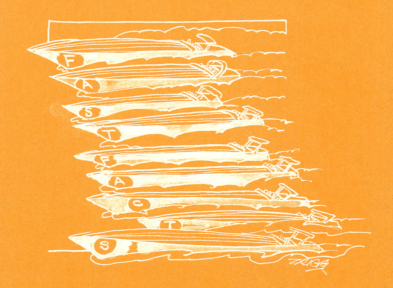

Life is boring without challenges, and I fully trust in my team's ability to meet their challenge and lead us to global excellence.

— His Highness Sheikh Mohammed bin Rashid Al Maktoum

Official Name
United Arab Emirates

Capital
Abu Dhabi

Flag
The UAE flag has three equal horizontal bands of green (top), white (middle) and black (bottom) with a wider vertical red band on the hoist side. Each color is shaped in a rectangular manner and looks similar to the letter E.

Red: Red represents hardiness, bravery, strength and courage. The vertical red band can also be interpreted as binding all the other meanings together in unity.

Green: Green represents hope, joy, optimism and love. It can also symbolise the country's prosperity.

White: White represents peace and honesty. White is the purest colour, and is interpreted by some to symbolise cleanliness.

Black: Contrary to popular belief, the black band does not represent oil. It stands for the defeat of enemies, and also strength of mind.

Time
Greenwich Mean Time plus 4 hours (GMT +0400)

Telephone Country Code
(971)

Climate
Dubai has a tropical desert climate because of its location within the Northern desert belt. Summers are extremely hot and humid, with an average high around 45 °C (113 °F) and overnight lows around 30 °C (86 °F).

Population
2.5 million (Dubai)

Language and Dialects
Arabic is the official language of UAE. Four major dialects of Arabic are widely used. Maghrebi Arabic, Egyptian Arabic, Gulf Arabic and Levantine Arabic. English is widely used around the city. Other languages more prominent in the city are Hindi, Urdu and Malayam.

Official Religion
Islam

Government
Federal, Presidential, Absolute Monarchy. The United Arab Emirates (UAE) is a federation of seven constituent monarchies: the Emirates of Abu Dhabi, Ajman,Dubai, Fujairah, Ras al-Khaimah, Sharjah, and Umm al-Quwain.

Currency
UAE Dirham (AED)

Industries
Petroleum and petrochemicals, fishing, aluminium, cement, fertilisers, commercial ship repair, construction materials, aerospace parts, financial services, tourism, pharmaceuticals, steel, handicrafts, textiles.

Exports
Crude oil, natural gas, reexports, dried fish, dates

Ethnic Groups
Local Emiratis (19 per cent), Arabs and Others (21 per cent), Asians (60 per cent)

Airports
Al Maktoum International Airport
Dubai International Airport (Terminals 1, 2 and 3)

Electricity
The electrical current in Dubai is 220/240 V, 50 Hz AC. British style 3-pin electrical plugs are used (Type G or 13 amp plug). Socket adaptors are easily available.

FAMOUS PEOPLE
Sheikh Rashid bin Saeed Al Maktoum
Sheikh Rashid, was the Vice President of the UAE from its founding, and Ruler of Dubai for 32 years. He is known as the Father of modern Dubai, transforming a small trading port into a major international shipping centre. The discovery of oil in the 1960s made it possible to expand port facilities

and construct an international airport. His understanding that Dubai needed an economy that would thrive beyond the emirate's limited oil reserves is expressed in his saying: "My grandfather rode a camel, my father rode a camel, I drive a Mercedes, my son drives a Land Rover, his son will drive a Land Rover, but his son will ride a camel."

His Highness Sheikh Mohammed bin Rashid Al Maktoum

On 4 January 2006, His Highness Sheikh Mohammed bin Rashid Al Maktoum became the Ruler of Dubai following the death of Sheikh Maktoum bin Rashid Al Maktoum. From 2007 onwards, Dubai has witnessed unique achievements under his leadership, including the launch of a nationwide philanthropic campaign called "Dubai Cares", opening of The Palm Jumeirah in 2008, Dubai Metro in 2009, opening of Burj Khalifa in 2010, winning Expo 2020 in 2013, launch of the Happiness Meter in 2014 and the launch of Al Amal (Hope), the Arab world's first Mars probe.

Crown Prince Sheikh Hamdan bin Mohammed bin Rashid Al Maktoum

Sheikh Hamdan, or Fazza, as he is fondly known, has been taking social media by storm, racking up over three million followers on Instagram and recently being chosen as one of the top 100 "global personalities" on Snapchat. An incredible athlete, Fazza took home the gold medal in a 160 km (99.4 mile) endurance ride after competing against a total of 227 riders, representing 41 countries. He is also a passionate freediver (a difficult form of underwater diving that relies on the diver's ability to hold their breath) and does everything from swimming and cycling to snowboarding, running and tennis. From wing walking, fly boarding, zip lining past the Burj, flying in an Airbus A380 next to Jet Man, taking a selfie from the top of the Burj Khalifa, diving with elephants, trekking on glaciers – if it sounds terrifying, Fazza has done it.

His Highness Sheikh Ahmed bin Saeed Al Maktoum

Over the past 25 years His Highness Sheikh Ahmed bin Saeed Al Maktoum has been at the forefront of Dubai's remarkable economic development spearheading the successful expansion of aviation and, more recently, formulating economic, investment and fiscal policies and strategies in support of the emirate's overarching vision.

In 1985, Sheikh Ahmed was appointed President of the Dubai Department of Civil Aviation (DCA) – the governing body that oversaw the activities of Dubai International and Dubai Duty Free, among others. In the same year Emirates Airline, Dubai's international carrier, was launched with Sheikh Ahmed as its Chairman. He is now the Chairman and Chief Executive of Emirates Airline and Group, which includes dnata – the region's leading travel services and ground handling company, and other aviation related entities. Sheikh Ahmed is also chairman of Dubai's biggest bank, Emirates NBD, and of Dubai World, the conglomerate that includes the world's third biggest ports company, DP World. Sheikh Ahmed is also the chairman of Dubai Airport Free Zone Authority, Dubai Air Wing, Alliance Insurance Company, The British University in Dubai, and The Dubai Power & Energy Committee. He is the chairman of Wasl Hospitality and chairman of Noor Investment Group and the chairman of Noor Takaful. Sheikh Ahmed is Commandeur de l'Ordre de la Légion d'honneur (the Legion of Honour) the highest French civilian award.

His Highness Sheikh Hamdan bin Rashid Al Maktoum

His Highness Sheikh Hamdan bin Rashid Al Maktoum, the second son of the late ruler, Rashid bin Saeed Al Maktoum, is the Deputy Ruler of Dubai and the Minister of Finance and Industry of the UAE. He graduated from Bell School of Languages, Cambridge, and is in charge of an array of key governmental industrial enterprises, including the Dubai Aluminium Company, Dubai Gas Company and Dubai Cable Company, among others. His other interests include thoroughbred horse racing.

Sheikha Lubna Al Qasimi

Sheikha Lubna Al Qasimi holds the distinction of being the first woman to hold a ministerial post in UAE. Currently holding the portfolio of Minister of State for Tolerance, Sheikha Lubna was previously Minister of State for International Cooperation and Minister of Economic and Planning, winning plaudits for developing a system that slashed cargo turnaround times at Dubai airport. In 2000 she founded Tejari, the Middle East's first business-to-business online marketplace. She has helped to lead the country into a period of unprecedented philanthropy, contributing to charities, volunteering with Friends of Cancer Patients Society and serving on the Board of Directors for the Dubai Autism Center. Graduating from the California State University with a Bachelor's Degree in Computer Science, she completed an EMBA degree from the American University of Sharjah. As of 2016, she is listed as the 43rd most powerful woman in the world by Forbes.

CULTURE QUIZ

SITUATION 1

You are invited to an Emirati home for Iftar during Ramadan. The food is all laid but you are not offered anything. You think:

Ⓐ How rude of the hosts to lay out the food and not offer anything to you.

Ⓑ You understand it is an Iftar and you will be offered food and drinks once its time to break the fast at Iftar once Adhan is heard.

Ⓒ You look at your host and smile with hope.

Comments

Ⓑ is correct. Ramadan is the Holy Month in the Islamic Calendar, when Muslims fast from sunrise to sunset for approximately 30 days. Fasting during Ramadan is one of the five pillars of Islam. The dates for Ramadan change annually as they're determined by the sighting of a new moon. The start and end of Ramadan will be declared the day before. The appropriate greeting is "Ramadan Kareem" which means "generous", so the expression means "Wish you generous Ramadan". Iftar is the meal to break the fast after sunset. Typically, people will enjoy dates, dried apricots and Ramadan juices, before heading to evening prayer. After that, large meals are the norm, usually with family and friends. Suhoor is a meal taken just before sunrise, before the day of fasting starts.

SITUATION 2

You are a male and female team going for a formal meeting with your Emirati business associates. You, the male, shakes hands with your business contacts. The Emirati female does not offer her hand for a handshake with you but does with your female team member. Do you:

A Take offence. Think she is not well versed with corporate etiquette.

B Understand and are aware that that Emirati women do not offer a handshake to men.

C Find it strange to be left out without a handshake.

Comments

B is correct. Emiratis are particularly polite and warm between the different sexes. A general greeting of "Salaam Waleikum", which translates as "peace be upon you". The proper etiquette of reply with "Waleikum assalaam", which means "and on you peace" goes a long way as an ice breaker and give a comfort level to your local associates.

You should always make a point of greeting each man in the room individually, starting of course with the host. For men, handshakes are the most common form of greeting. However, although a firm handshake is commonplace and seen as a sign of friendliness and trust in the West, in the UAE a handshake is gentle. In more relaxed circumstances, women may kiss each other on the cheek.

It is extremely important to remember that you should only ever shake hands with your right hand. The left hand is considered unclean, as traditionally it is thought to be used for more unsanitary purposes! Therefore, whether you're shaking hands, eating, offering or taking something, the proper etiquette is to always use your right hand only.

SITUATION 3

You have made new friends in Dubai and have invited them

over to your home. You offer them alcohol and they ask for a glass of juice. You think:

Ⓐ Your new friend is rude in not accepting your offer for a drink.

Ⓑ You are confused why someone would like a juice when you are offering a drink.

Ⓒ You are aware Muslims do not consume alcohol. You respect the local culture and join your friend's choice of juice.

Comments

Ⓒ is correct. While alcohol is served in some hotels and sold in a few designated stores, it may generally only be purchased by people who hold a liquor license in Dubai. These licenses are valid only in the emirate that issued the license.

Liquor licenses are only issued to people who possess current UAE residency permits and who are non-Muslim. Just about any public activity that you can think of that involves alcohol is illegal. There is zero tolerance for drinking and driving in Dubai. Passengers in transit through the UAE under the influence of alcohol may also be arrested.

SITUATION 4

You go for a swim to the beach, enjoy the sun and are now ready for some lunch. You put on your lace top and micro minis and and decide to grab some lunch from the nearby mall. You are stopped by a mall official for inappropriate dressing and are guided to the mall entrance where the dress code is stated. You think:

Ⓐ Why is there so much fuss about a lace top? After all, it looks nice on you and you don't understand why you are picked upon by the mall official.

Ⓑ It is so hot in Dubai. You want to wear as little clothes as possible.

🄲 You apologise and go home to change.

Comments

🄲 is correct. Emiratis dress conservatively in traditional dress and can be offended when people dress inappropriately or not in accordance with Islamic values. In public places such as shopping malls, restaurants and parks, you are encouraged to dress appropriately. Clothing should not be transparent, indecently expose parts of the body or display offensive pictures or slogans. Be aware that if you enter one of these areas dressed inappropriately you may be asked to leave (most of the larger shopping malls display signs warning that respectable clothing should be worn). Any form of nudity is strictly forbidden, including topless sunbathing. Swimwear should not be worn in any other area outside the beach, water parks, or swimming pools.

SITUATION 5

You and your partner have just landed from Europe to Dubai. You are kissing at the airport. You are frowned on and told to stop by another local at the airport. You:

🄐 Think this is confusing. You are partners and this is normal.
🄑 Ask for an explanation.
🄒 Apologise and understand that you are in an Islamic country.

Comments

🄒 is correct. Displays of affection among couples, whether married or not, in public places does not fit into the local customs and culture of Dubai. Holding hands for a married couple is tolerated but kissing and petting are considered an offence to public decency. If you are caught you could be fined and imprisoned.

DO'S AND DON'TS

DO'S

Travelling

- Do take your best camera to Dubai. It has several spots you will love to see again and again.
- Be careful of what you carry and save yourself some serious trouble. Only one month's supply of controlled and restricted medicine can be brought into Dubai. For non-controlled prescription medicine, up to three months' supply can be brought in. For a complete list of the banned drugs log on to the Ministry of Health (MOH) official website: www.moh.gov.ae
- Do enjoy your stay in Dubai but keep a check on the expiry date of your visa.

Living

- Tipping is accepted in taxis, hotels and restaurants.
- Do wear the bikini to the beach. However, be mindful of not wearing any swim wear or inappropriate clothing in public places.

DON'TS

Travelling

- Don't take pictures of women without their permission.
- Do not overstay as this leads to fines upon exit.

Living

- Don't share your apartment in the person of the opposite sex unless you are married or are a blood relative. The law forbids live-in arrangements and it is considered illegal. Don't be surprised if you landlord asks you to submit a marriage certificate if you are planning to share your apartment with your partner.

- Do not show any offensive behaviour, language, or rude hand gestures. These are viewed very seriously and can result in imprisonment and deportation. This is considered "road rage".

- Do not drink and drive. This can land you in trouble with the authorities.

- Public displays of affection is something not taken too well in the city. Several cases in the past have ended in legal action.

- Do not show any disrespect for any particular community or religion. Dubai is a very tolerant society.

- Do not attempt to cross dress in Dubai. Men dressing as women are subject to prosecution. While this may be accepted in the Western world, cross dressing has zero tolerance in Dubai society and leads to deportations and even fines or prison.

GLOSSARY

LANGUAGE

THE BASICS	ARABIC	SIMPLIFIED ARABIC
Hello	Ahlan Wa Sahlan	اهلا وسهلا
Thank You	Shukran	شكرا
Good Bye	Ma Assalam	ام السلام
Man	Rajul	رجل
Woman	Imra	امرأة
No Problem	La Mushkila	لا مشكلة
Take Care	Aietann Binafsik	اعتن بنفسك
Is That Right?	Hal Hadha Sahih	هل هذه صحيح
Do You Want It?	Hal Turiduh	هل تريده
Sorry	A'asif	أصف
Not Bad	Laisa Sayiyaan	ليس سيئا

NUMBERS

Zero	Sifar	صفر
One	Waahid	واحد
Two	Ithnaan	أثنان
Three	Thalatha	ثالثة
Four	Arba'a	أربع
Five	Khamsa	خمسة
Six	Sitta	ستة
Seven	Saba	سبع
Eight	Thamania	ثمانية
Nine	Tisa'a	تسعة
Ten	Ashra	عشرة

COUNTRIES

ENGLISH	ARABIC	SIMPLIFIED ARABIC
Australia	Astralia	استراليا
Canada	Canada	كندا
China	As-Seen	الصين
Denmark	Ad-Danmarik	الدنمارك
England	Inkaltara	انكلترا
Europe	Orobba	اوروبا
France	Faransa	فرنسا
Germany	Almaania	ألمانيا
Holland	Hollanda	هولندا
Hong Kong	Hong Kong	هونغ كونغ
Ireland	Irlanda	أيرلندا
Italy	Italia	ايطاليا
Japan	Al-Yabaan	اليابان
Korea	Korea	كوريا
Mongolia	Mongolia	منغوليا
Scotland	Iskotlanda	اسكوتلندا
Singapore	Singafora	سنغافورة
Sweden	Al-Suwed	السويد
South Africa	Junoob Afrikia	جنوب أفريقيا
Switzerland	Suisra	سويسرا
Tibet	Al-Tabt	التبت
United States	Alwilayaat Almuttahida	الولايات المتحدة
Gate	Al-Baab	الباب
Outside	Khaarij	خارج
Inside	Daakhil	داخل

English	Arabic	Say it in English
East	Mashrik	مشرق
West	Maghrib	مغرب
North	Shimaal	شمال
South	Junoob	جنوب

ENGLISH	ARABIC	SAY IT IN ENGLISH
January	يَناير	Yanayir
February	فبْرايِر	Fibrayir
March	مارِس	Maris
April	أبَرْيل	Abril
May	مايو	Mayu
June	يونيو	Yunuyu
July	يوليو	Yuliyu
August	أغُسْطُس	Aghustus
September	سبْتَمْبِر	Sibtambir
October	أكْتوبِر	Uktabar
November	نوفَمْبِر	Nufambir
December	ديسَمْبِر	Disambir

ISLAMIC MONTHS

The Islamic calendar, Muslim calendar or Hijri calendar (Anno Hijri or AH) is a lunar calendar consisting of 12 months in a year of 354 or 355 days. It contains 12 months that are based on the motion of the moon, and because 12 Synodic months is only 12 x 29.53 = 354.36 days, the Islamic calendar is consistently shorter than a tropical year, and therefore shifts with respect to the christian calendar.

مُحَرَّم	Mulharram
صَفَر	Safar
رَبيع الأوّل	Rabi Al-Awwal
رَبيع الثاني \ الآخِر	Rabi Al-Thani/Al-Akhir
جُمادى الأولى \ الأوّل	Jumada I-Ula/I-Awwal
جُمادى الثانِية \ الآخِرة	Jumada I-Thaniya/I-Akhira
رَجَب	Rajab
شَعْبان	Shaaban
رَمَضان	Ramadan
شَوّال	Shawwal
ذو القَعْدة	Dhu Al-Qada
ذو الحجّة	Dhu Al-Hijja

RESOURCE GUIDE

To make international calls, dial 00, followed by the international code.

EMERGENCY NUMBERS

- Police   999
- Ambulance and air rescue   999
- Fire department   997
- Electricity & water   991
- Dubai Municipality Emergency 04-2232323
- Tourist security   800 4888
- Road services (AAA)   800 4430
- Al Ameen (to report criminal
  activity or harassment)   800 4888 (tel)
                                              800 4444 (text)

AIRLINES AND AIRPORTS

- Dubai International Airport   04-2245555
- Flight Information   04-2166666
- Emirates Airlines   04-2144444

USEFUL WEBSITES

- www.dubai.ae/en/Pages/Default.aspx
- www.visitdubai.com
- www.timeout dubai.com

FOREIGN EMBASSIES AND CONSULATES

Refer to www.embassy.goabroad.com/embassies-in/united-arab-emirates

HOSPITALS

- **Latifaa Hospital**   04-2193000
- **American Hospital**   04-3096645
- **Dubai Hospital**   04-2195000
- **Al Baraha Hospital**   04-2710000
- **Rashid Hospital**   04-2192000
- **Welcare Hospita**   04-2829900
- **Jebel Ali Hospital**   04-8845666
- **Iranian Hospital**   04-3440250
- **Belhoul Specialty Hospital** 04-2733333
- **Medcare Hospital**   04-4079100
- **Canadian Specialist Hospital** 04-3364444
- **The City Hospital**   800 8432489
- **Cedars Jebel Ali Hospital**   04-8814000
- **Neuro Spinal Hospital**   04-3157887
- **Zulekha Hospital**   04-2678866

SCHOOLS

The Knowledge and Human Development Authority (KHDA) is responsible for the growth and quality of private education in Dubai. The school inspection reports published in www.khda. gov.ae from 2009 to 2015 provide a comprehensive review of the performance and standards of private schools in Dubai in general, and of every private school in Dubai in particular. The information contained in the reports is designed to assist parents' work more closely with schools, as partners in their children's learning, and facilitates school improvement. The Dubai School Inspections Bureau encourages school leaders to share their improvement and action plans with parents when inspection reports are published. For details of schools and individual school reports, refer to: www.khda.gov.ae/en.

CLUBS

- **India Club**

  Call: 04-33771112

- **Pakistan Club**

  Call: 04-3373632

- **Jordanian Club**

  Call: 04-3371770

- **Egyptian Club**

  Call: 04-3366709

- **Iranian Club**

  Call: 04-3367700

- **Sudanese Club**

  Call: 04-3371294

- **Dubai Polo and Equestrian Club**

  Call: 04-3618111

- **Rotary Club of Dubai**

  Call: 04-3251666

- **Dubai International Seafarers Club**

  Call: 04-3576060

- **Jebel Ali Shooting Club**

  Call: 04-8836555

SERVICES

- **Dubai Electricity and Water Authority** (DEWA)

  www.dewa.ae

- **Visas**

  www.dnrd.ae

- **Phones and Internet**

  www.etisalat.ae

  www.du.ae

- **Ordering in:**
  www.foodonclick.com
  www.talabat.com
- **Tickets**
  www.ticketmaster.ae

CLASSIFIEDS
www.souq.com
www.dubizzle.com
www.yellowpages.ae
www.Jadopado.com
www.namshi.com

EVENTS AND ACTIVITIES
www.Dubaicalendar.ae
www.dubaiparksandresorts.com

NEWSPAPERS
www.gulfnews.com
www.khaleejtimes.com
www.emirates247.com

RADIO
www.virginradioDubai.com

WOMEN'S GUIDE
www.expatwoman.com/Dubai

VOLUNTEER ORGANISATIONS
AdoptaCamp is an initiative to meaningfully improve the lives of the men who built the beautiful cities we live in, and through

them, to reach out to and aid the diverse communities they come from. Email: adoptacamp@gmail.com

In **SmartAdopt** a white collar office worker adopts a blue collar worker. The mentor calls the labourer or the adopted person once a week and speaks to him/her.

Aid in Motion, in partnership with the Dubai Charity Association and Aramex, aims at collecting unwanted second hand clothing in Dubai and redistributing the collections in less advantaged areas of the city, primarily labour camps in Sonapur although they hope to soon expand their distribution areas. Tel: (971) 4870-6535.

The Centre serves children with special needs from different nationalities. The centre is always looking for volunteers to help out in any way they can. Email: alnoorspneeds@alnooruae.org

The Christina Noble Children's Foundation (CNCF) is dedicated to helping children in need through education, medical care, social opportunities, and job placement in Vietnam and Mongolia. Email: dubai@cncf.org

The Dubai Animal Rescue Centre (DARC) is a Dubai based sanctuary dedicated to the rescue, treatment, care and welfare of lost, abandoned and injured animals. Including exotics, birds, reptiles, equine, rodents and more. Email: info@darcuae.org

Dubai Autism Center provides specialist services for people with autism and those who care for them. Volunteers are always welcome to provide help and support for individuals with autism. Volunteers are essential part of the successful delivery of services at DAC. Email: info@dubaiautismcenter.ae

The Emirates Arthritis Foundation (EAF) is a non-profit organisation that contributes to the welfare of the entire region by providing an extensive range of events and programmes to support arthritis patients.Email: info@arthritis.ae

Feline Friends – If you care about the welfare of cats and kittens and want to support the never-ending work they do, please consider volunteering and/or making a donation. Email: newvolunteers@felinefriendsdubai.com

Gulf for Good has four main objectives which are to bring together Gulf nationals and residents for a good cause; to encourage people to push their own limits; to show people the value and enjoyment of motivation, commitment and helping others; and to raise large sums for worthwhile projects. Email: admin@gulf4good.org

Take My Junk is a private business that is run by a Canadian family who saw a need in the community to reduce waste and help lower income labourers and families by re-using unwanted items of furniture from residents leaving Dubai or the UAE. Take My Junk has re-used thousands of items from the rich to the poor. Email: info@takemyjunkuae.com

Dubai Offshore Sailing Club (DOSC) The Sailability programme is committed to giving people with disabilities the opportunity to learn to sail and they offer a structured sailing programme to students from special needs schools.

Sailability's activities are designed to introduce and encourage people to participate in sailing activities in a safe and supportive environment, with Bronze, Silver and Gold Certificates of Achievement to mark progress. The Sailability programme is primarily supported by DOSC and is run entirely by volunteers. Email: administration@doscuae.com

START is a non-profit organisation which applies the universal language of art to heal, educate and enrich the skills and opportunities of children in the poorest areas of the Middle East. In the UAE, START runs workshops for children with special needs including autism and Down Syndrome. Email: nicola@startworld.org

Volunteer in Dubai brings together any organisation, good cause or individual effort in the UAE, with people willing to help out. Even if only for one hour and even if it's infrequent, it makes an enormous difference. Volunteers are always needed. Email: info@volunteerinuae.com

BOOKSTORES
- Book Corner LLC: Gate No.2, Offfice 138, Dubai 04-3242442
- Magrudy Enterprises LLC: Magrudy's Mall, Jumeirah 1, Dubai 04-3444193
- Booksplus - Town Centre Shop # FF 15-16, Town Centre, Jumeirah Beach Road, 04-3442008
- The Book Worm Bookshop: Park and Shop Centre, Al Wasl Road, Jumeirah Dubai, 04-3945770

FURTHER READING

The Dubai that you see is a vision of His Highness Sheikh Mohammed bin Rashid Al Maktoum. Read his book called *Flashes of Thought* to get an insight into his dreams, aspirations and vision of Dubai. *Flashes of Thought* is a compilation of His Highness Sheikh Mohammed bin Rashid Al Maktoum's ideas about leadership and governance and covers several topic about leadership, creative thinking, positivity, his personal life, success and the drivers.

40 Poems From the Desert is another great collection of his old and new poems which His Highness Sheikh Mohammed bin Rashid Al Maktoum signed at the opening ceremony of Burj Khalifa.

Camels Love Dubai, by Stephen Wilkins is a good read. It is the story of Mohan Adikaram from Sri Lanka who loses his family in the 2004 tsunami. He moves to Dubai and attends university after being fostered or sponsored by a rich Dubai resident.

ABOUT THE AUTHOR

Leena Asher

Leena Asher is from the third generation of an Indian family in Dubai. Her grandfather arrived at the shores of Dubai from Karachi (which was then a part of India) in a ship called "Launch", covering a distance of 1,158 km (720 miles) in a week. Her father, Naraindas Asher, has since set up his home and business in Dubai. His business thrives in Deira's bustling Baniyas market even today.

Having completed all her education up to a post-graduate level in Dubai, she has complete faith in the quality of education that Dubai has to offer.

Dubai is her home and this is where she will always want to live. She has travelled the globe with her husband, Sanaullah Khan, a renowned Dubai-based businessman and the backbone of her achievements and considers Dubai as home because it provides safety and security to her family and a quality of life that she sees unmatched. Her children Vikrant and Viraj were both born and raised in Dubai. The fourth generation of her family now lives in Dubai, because they believe in the leadership of Dubai and the quality of life people enjoy in Dubai.

She works as a senior analyst in a company in the energy sector and is involved in various voluntary causes around the city. She loves art and music.

INDEX

A

abaya 10, 24, 33, 43
abra 15, 120, 124, 125, 84, 148
accommodation 35, 58, 119
agal 10
Atlantis 25, 121

B

Banking 49, 65, 66, 67, 74, 75
bisht 11
blood money 90
Bur Dubai 14, 15, 25, 31, 57, 59, 84, 113, 120, 123, 124, 126, 127, 129, 148, 151, 170
Burj Al Arab 21, 111, 120, 121
Burj Khalifa 45, 111, 120, 121, 142, 212, 213, 232

C

camel 10, 11, 27, 109, 120, 153, 154, 157, 165, 168, 169, 212
coffee 11, 12, 111, 115, 116, 117, 124
consulate 53, 54, 100, 101, 104
costs of living 76
crime 4, 65, 90, 103

D

Deira 14, 15, 25, 31, 59, 84, 120, 123, 124, 125, 126, 129, 170, 233
DIAC 82
DIFC 15, 18, 158
domestic help 159
driver's license 85, 86
Dubai Creek 14, 20, 25, 151
Dubai Land Department 57, 61
Dubai Mall 120, 122, 128, 129, 156, 167
Dubai Marina 15, 16, 17, 59, 84, 119, 132, 157
Dubai Plan 2021 45, 46
Dubai World Cup 143, 169
Dubai World Trade Centre 145, 185
Dune Bashing 87

E

economy 46, 195, 196, 212
education 43, 46, 77, 81, 82, 97, 146, 176, 182, 192, 194, 197, 198, 206, 226, 229, 233

Eid Al-Adha 131
Eid Al-Fitr 131
embassy 53, 54, 100, 101, 225
Emirates Airlines 21, 40, 41, 42, 136, 196, 225
Emirates Towers 135, 136
Emiratis 4, 11, 29, 30, 32, 38, 42, 43, 46, 79, 93, 99, 111, 115, 117, 131, 183, 191, 211, 216, 218
employment residence visa 52
events 4, 12, 41, 130, 133, 134, 135, 136, 143, 145, 149, 151, 153, 155, 161, 172, 230
expatriate 30, 32, 36, 39, 40, 49, 63, 76, 100, 104, 106, 109, 171, 172, 191, 193, 194, 197, 198, 199, 200, 203
Expo 2020 21, 30, 45, 212

G

galleries 18, 133, 138, 158
ghutra 10, 11, 33
Gold Souq 120, 122, 123, 125, 126, 129
Gulf Co-operation Council 2

H

health care 93
His Highness Sheikh Ahmed bin Saeed Al Maktoum 213
His Highness Sheikh Hamdan bin Rashid Al Maktoum 214
His Highness Sheikh Mohammed Bin Rashid Al Maktoum 2, 22, 209
His Highness Sheikh Zayed bin Sultan Al Nahyan 4

I

Iftar 93, 130, 141, 215
insurance 49, 50, 51, 65, 72, 75, 79, 91, 93, 95, 96, 105, 162, 163, 198
Islamic calendar 224

J

Jebel Ali port 26, 196
Jumeirah 14, 15, 16, 17, 21, 25, 26, 27, 57, 59, 60, 84, 111, 135, 136, 138, 139, 143, 147, 157, 158, 212, 231
Jumeirah Beach Residence 16, 59, 143
Jumeirah Lake 17, 59

K

kandoora 10, 11
KHDA 81, 82, 226
kids 63, 89, 133, 135, 149, 156, 167, 175

L

language 4, 5, 31, 68, 181, 182, 183, 184, 185, 191, 210, 220, 231
liquor permit 55, 106

M

majlis 22, 34, 35, 115, 148
Majlis Gallery 15, 133
Mall of the Emirates 84, 88, 122, 128
Metro 6, 7, 21, 84, 85, 122, 140, 163, 212
Minister of Happiness 23, 24

N

Nol 5, 6, 84

O

Ottoman Empire 20
oud 115, 116, 117, 126
Oud Metha 25, 27, 31, 57, 59, 110, 150, 158

P

Palm Jumeirah 21, 25, 26, 84, 212
Palm Monorail 84
Palms 25
Persian Gulf 24, 25, 119
pets 9, 51, 63, 64
property 39, 56, 57, 58, 59, 60, 61, 140, 176

R

Ramadan 32, 35, 82, 93, 123, 129, 130, 131, 141, 142, 189, 191, 199, 215, 224
Ras Al Khor 113, 150, 158
religion 26, 33, 74, 105, 116, 158, 187, 191, 220
Rental 58, 59, 91
RERA 57, 61
restaurant 108, 109, 148, 161
RTA 68, 83, 84, 85, 86, 92, 93, 169

S

Sharia law 74, 75, 76, 103
shawarma 108, 110, 127, 158
Sheikha Lubna Al Qasimi 214
Sheikh Hamdan bin Mohammed bin Rashid Al Maktoum 212
Sheikh Mohammed Centre for Cultural Understanding 132
Sheikh Rashid bin Saeed Al Maktoum 211
Sheikh Saeed house 151, 152
Sheikh Zayed Road 7, 14, 25, 88, 127, 187
sheila 10, 33, 43
Smart Dubai 24
Spice Souq 125, 126
sports 4, 83, 94, 136, 141, 144, 145, 168, 173, 174, 175

T

tax 36, 74, 75, 122, 161, 198
Tea and Coffee Festival 12
telecommunications 80
temperature 7, 8, 11, 80, 154
Textile Souq 126
The Greens 18
The Universe 25
The Waterfront 25
The World 25
tipping 219

U

UAE 12, 18, 20, 22, 23, 24, 26, 31, 36, 39, 44, 45, 52, 58, 74, 75, 76, 80, 86, 88, 100, 101, 103, 104, 122, 131, 133, 134, 140, 142, 143, 147, 154, 158, 168, 183, 184, 185, 187, 188, 190, 203, 204, 206, 207, 209, 210, 211, 214, 216, 217, 230, 231
Umayyad Caliphate 20

V

volunteers 207, 229, 231

W

wedding 33, 98, 99, 100, 101

Titles in the CultureShock! series:

Argentina	Germany	Philippines
Australia	Great Britain	Portugal
Austria	Greece	Russia
Bahrain	Hawaii	San Francisco
Beijing	Hong Kong	Saudi Arabia
Belgium	Hungary	Scotland
Berlin	India	Sri Lanka
Bolivia	Ireland	Shanghai
Borneo	Italy	Singapore
Bulgaria	Jakarta	South Africa
Brazil	Japan	Spain
Cambodia	Korea	Sri Lanka
Canada	Laos	Sweden
Chicago	London	Switzerland
Chile	Malaysia	Syria
China	Mauritius	Taiwan
Costa Rica	Morocco	Thailand
Cuba	Munich	Tokyo
Czech Republic	Myanmar	Travel Safe
Denmark	Netherlands	Turkey
Ecuador	New Zealand	United Arab Emirates
Egypt	Norway	USA
Finland	Pakistan	Vancouver
France	Paris	Venezuela

For more information about any of these titles, please contact any of our Marshall Cavendish offices around the world (listed on page ii) or visit our website at:

www.marshallcavendish.com/genref